*Lynn,*
*May every day inspire you!*
*With blessings,*
*Burhans*

# Good Night and God Bless

## Celebrating Love, Laughter
## and the Lessons of Loss

Linda Burhans

Breath & Shadows Productions
Tampa, FL

ISBN-13: 978-0-9821029-0-9

Cover design by Jennifer Travis, Travis Design & Print,
St. Petersburg, FL

Printed in the United States of America

Breath & Shadows Productions
P.O. Box 10557, Tampa FL 33679
813.251.8187
www.breathandshadows.com

# Good Night and God Bless

*Celebrating Love, Laughter*

*and the Lessons of Loss*

*For the woman who taught me, listened to me, and loved me. Mama, thank you for all you continued to teach me after I learned to tie my shoes.*

*And to my daughter Nicole (aka Nickadeemis). My life was blessed and brightened immensely the day you were born. I have always loved you and always will, just like Grandma.*

# Contents

# In the Beginning...

My first memory is of a crisp, refreshing day in 1956, outside our home in Woodhaven, Queens, New York. I rode my red tricycle up the driveway and stepped up the two brick steps into the side door of our apartment. There was my mom in the warm, brightly lit kitchen, cooking chocolate pudding on the stove. I don't know what was more wonderful ... my beautiful, smiling mommy or the delicious smell of the pudding. I do remember it was all good.

Mommy, Daddy, and I lived in a two-family apartment house in a middle-class neighborhood, where I remember all our neighbors were really nice people. I especially liked the man next door. He had a basement full of peanuts and hot pretzels that he sold from a cart on the corner.

I also remember our landlord. Mrs. Reggio was not nice. She was mean. She was always complaining to

*Even at age three, the world was my oyster—and Mama was its pearl.*

somebody about something. She lived upstairs above us and constantly watched every move I made from her window. One day my friend Jane and I were outside, digging in the next door garden with a spoon. We were having a wonderful time when all of a sudden we heard Mrs. Reggio yelling—and my name was included in what she was yelling.

Jane and I tiptoed into the side door of our apartment and, through the kitchen, we could see Mrs. Reggio in my living room, yelling at my mommy. She was yelling that I had dug up her flowers, and my mother had better watch out for me. My mom was pregnant at the time and she began to cry.

That made me mad! I ran into the living room, climbed up on the arm of our big sofa, and told that awful lady, "Don't you yell at my mommy! Don't you make my mommy cry!" Mrs. Reggio left promptly, in a huff. I don't remember ever seeing her again.

That night when my daddy came home from work, my mommy told him what had happened that afternoon. I remember him taking me on his lap and telling me how proud he was of me. I also distinctly remember his words, "Always love Mommy and take care of her."

And that, I believe, is when my infatuation with Mama really began.

# New York, New York

*I live by this credo:*
*Have a little laugh at life and look around you for*
*happiness instead of sadness. Laughter has always*
*brought me out of unhappy situations.*
Red Skelton

*December 29, 2005*

   Mom left this morning after visiting for nine days.
It was really nice to have her here, especially since we
haven't spent a Christmas Day together since I moved
to Florida five years ago. It was a glorious day and all the
way to the airport Mom talked about the sunshine and
the beautiful clouds. The airport was a little busy as I
checked her in at the terminal counter, but Mom assured
me I didn't have to take her to the gate. I kissed

her goodbye, gave her a big hug, and told her to call me when she got home. Tears filled my eyes as I watched her board the tram for the gate. I noticed Mom is really beginning to age. I worry about her.

Although I always tell her to call me when she arrives home, she usually forgets. So when I called this evening and there was no answer I was quite surprised. After a few phone calls I discovered Mom's flight had been cancelled due to bad weather in New York. She sat in the Tampa airport for almost seven hours all by herself and never called me! Mom is definitely not as sharp as she used to be.

I just sent her the following e-mail: *Dear Mom—I am sorry you had such a difficult time getting home. If you had called me, I would have come and picked you up. I think you didn't call because you didn't have any phone numbers with you. I have listed below all of our phone numbers. Please print this out and keep it in your wallet or purse. I will also mail you a prepaid calling card that you can use at any phone. I love you,*

*When one door of happiness closes, another opens; but often we look so long at the closed door that we do not see the one which has been opened for us.*
Helen Keller

*January 6, 2006*

It was a cold, miserable, gray day as my plane landed at John F. Kennedy International Airport. I must be out of my mind coming to New York in January. Even the airline stewardess—or whatever they call themselves these days, questioned whether we really wanted to leave warm, sunny Tampa this morning.

I am here for a good reason, though. Mom has finally agreed to sell her house and move into some kind of a senior community. For at least ten years my sisters and brother and I have been trying to convince her to sell that big house in West Hempstead. It's a three-story English Tudor and Mom will gladly tell you it has four doors and thirty-two windows that she has cleaned time and time again. She will also tell you she has lived there for forty-nine years, and that she doesn't like change. She will add that this is the only place she knows and that she loves her church. But the house is falling down around her. She is not able to take care of it any longer, physically or financially. Even if the house were in good shape—which it isn't—the property taxes, insurance, and fuel costs are much more than Mom can afford.

I have had visions for the five years I've been in Florida of someone calling to tell me that Mom fell down the rickety basement stairs and had been lying there for days. Although she is basically healthy, she does seem to fall often. Sometimes Mom doesn't see anyone for days, other than the people at daily Mass. My sister Pat lives on Long Island, about an hour from Mom, while our sister Stephanie is in Chester, New York, and our brother David is in Bayside, Queens. We all love Mom and worry about her.

I can't believe how cold it is here and now it's raining. Waiting on the airport curb for Stephanie to pick me up, people were bustling all around, hailing cabs, dragging luggage. I don't think one of them was smiling. I stood there wishing Mom would just move to Florida. With the weather so much nicer, she would be able to get out more and start to live again.

She barely leaves the house anymore, except to go to church each day and maybe once a week for some kind of church volunteer work. A couple of times a month she'll go to the movies, but almost always by herself. On Thursdays she drives into Howard Beach, Queens to visit my aunt Margie. My aunt Lee and uncle Walter meet there also. They usually go food shopping for Aunt Margie and then out to lunch. Aunt Margie has Alzheimer's and several other medical problems. There is an aide with her during the day, as she does nothing except lay on the couch these days. Mom has asked me, repeatedly, "If that ever happens to me, you will take care of me, right?"

"Of course I will, Mama."

"Promise me you'll never put me in a nursing home."

"Never, Mama. I promise."

When Stephanie pulled up and honked the horn, I jumped into her warm car. I was so glad to see her. We headed off to Mom's house to pick up our sister Pat and then to check out some senior communities for Mom.

We know Mom would like to stay in West Hempstead, as she does not want to leave her church or the neighborhood. Unfortunately, there is no place for her in West Hempstead. Pat had checked out some places in Lynbrook, not too far from Mom's house. She could still drive to church in West Hempstead if she wanted to.

Mom decided that she did not want to go with us and would leave the decision up to the three of us. Great. Not really. This was a big decision.

This is all so strange for me. My mother has always been strong, vibrant, and self-sufficient. In my mind, I always expected her to live in that big, old house until the day she died.

We visited a couple of places. The one we thought would be best was a new assisted living facility in

Lynbrook. Mom would have her own apartment. She could cook for herself or they offered restaurant-style service. There was a common area with a library, computer center, hair salon, spa, and media room. And they had all sorts of scheduled activities, from dancing to shopping to the theatre. It was clean and bright and it didn't have any "old people's" smell. The residents were lively, and the staff very accommodating and highly trained. The staff seemed to know all the residents by name, and I liked that. It was the sort of place where she could again become known as vibrant and active Jo McCauley, rather than just "Mom," "Aunt Jo," or "Grandma." My sisters and I talked and then called my brother. With David in agreement, we put down a $500 deposit and went home to tell Mom.

When we got back to the house, Mom seemed very quiet. She is definitely not the quiet type, especially when her three daughters are around. We told her all about the residential community and how wonderful it was going to be for her. She wouldn't be far from her church, she would have her own apartment, but there would always be things to do if she wanted to.

Mom sat there and didn't say a thing. Then suddenly, with a little smirk on her face, she said, "I'm not moving there. I'm moving to Florida."

*People of character do the right thing, not because they
think it will change the world but because they refuse
to be changed by the world.*
Michael Josephson

*January 10, 2006*

Mama is *really* going to move here. I can't believe it.
I called Daddy. Even though he and Mom have been
divorced for more than thirty years, we are all still really
close.

"What do you think, Dad?" I asked.

"I think it is good, Linda," he said clearly. That in
itself was amazing because most of the time it is difficult
for Daddy to speak clearly, due to a series of strokes and
other illnesses he's had.

"Ya think so, Dad?" I asked nervously.

"Yes Linda. You, you love your mo-, mo-, mother."
His words began to slur.

"Okay then. Say a prayer for me."

"We will, my darling," Heidi, Dad's wife, said.

Whenever I speak to them, they are both on the

phone, on two extensions. That way if Daddy has a problem with his speech, Heidi can decipher it. And she is a genie at it. If we ever play "Charades," I want Heidi to be my partner.

*March 8, 2006*

I got a call from my girlfriend Maureen this morning. Actually, she is my sister—not by blood, but she *is* my sister. My mom jokes that she had five kids, and Maureen was the only one who wasn't a pain to deliver and that she didn't have to potty train. Maureen and I have been friends since fifth grade. We have loved each other, disagreed with each other, disappointed, forgiven, understood and misunderstood each other, and we've laughed and cried with each other.

She was crying when she called. "I need to see you right now," she said. "I need to talk to you. Can you come to my office right now?"

When I arrived a few minutes later, she met me in the reception office.

"Are you sure it is best for your mother to move here, Linda Sue?" she demanded, and she started crying again. Maureen is one of the few people that will call me Linda Sue. And when she does, she is either joking around or very, very upset. It was quite obvious she was not joking around. One thing I know about Maureen is that she loves me from the bottom of her heart or, as she would say, "from the moon and back again!" That goes ditto for my daughter, grandchildren, and my mama.

"What are you talking about?" I asked.

"Your schedule is busier than busy. Are you going to have time for her? How are you going to 'fit her in,' Linda? Are you sure you are doing the right thing? I love your mother! Are you *sure* you are doing the right thing?" By then she was so upset she was sobbing.

After about twenty minutes, I think I convinced her I am doing the right thing, and that I will do whatever is needed to make my mama feel loved and comfortable. But as I pulled out of the parking lot, Maureen's words kept echoing in my head: "Are you doing the right thing, Linda Sue?"

*Can I really do this?*, I wondered. Can I make mom's life better? Or happier or more comfortable?

I know the answer: *Yes, you can, Linda Sue! Yes, you can! And* will.


*April 13, 2006*

Today is Mom's 77th birthday. Mama was named Josephine because she was born on the birthday of her father—Joseph.

Mom isn't supposed to be spending her birthday in Winthrop University Hospital in Mineola, New York. She is having a stent put in. Pat says a stent is a pretty routine procedure for heart trouble these days and that Mom will be fine. I am grateful my sister is a nurse, because medicine is definitely not my forte. I just told Pat, "Make sure Mama is all healthy when you send her down here. I'm good at entertaining but not doctor stuff."

April 13 is also the date my dad had his first stroke, in 2001. That day was the first time I ever thought about my parents' mortality. Didn't like thinking about it then, don't like thinking about it now. Yes, I am a true McCauley.

*June 17, 2006*

Mom's flight arrives at Tampa Airport tonight at 10:10 P.M. I am excited and at the same time apprehensive. Mom will now be my responsibility. I love her from the bottom of my heart but sometimes she does make me crazy. If she starts any of the negative stuff, I will just kill her with kindness.

I have been teaching her about where she will be living.

"Where are you moving to?" I ask.

"Florida."

"What town?"

"Seminole."

"What county is it in?"

"Pinellas."

"Where is that in Florida?"

"On the west coast."

"Good, Mama."

# *"Arrive Alive"*
# *—And Livin' Large!*

*June 18, 2006*

Last night as I drove to the airport to pick up Mama, my mind was reeling. In fact, my whole life with her was flashing before my eyes. I really could not believe she was actually moving to Florida. She always says that she hates it here and that she hates the heat.

I arrived at the gate with a bouquet of daisies and yellow roses. Mom loves yellow roses. She always had beautiful rose bushes in her garden—yellow, coral, white, and an especially gorgeous red velvet one right by the back gate. When in bloom, you could smell its beautiful aroma as you entered the yard.

I also had a sign, with a little pink flamingo, that read 'Welcome Home.' People kept standing in front of my sign. I wanted to yell at them to *get out of the way!* I watched as the passengers came off the tram from the plane. You can always tell the New Yorkers at the airport. Their skin is pale, and probably twenty-five percent of them have a New York Yankee logo on some article of clothing or luggage.

Where was Mama? Finally I spotted her, wearing her signature turtleneck shirt, a sweatshirt, and stirrup pants. I was thinking, *We've got to do something about your wardrobe, Mom, or you will die of heat stroke here.* She looked tired as she walked into the terminal. I could see her eyes scanning all the faces, looking for me. Once she spotted me, she broke out in a big smile. I ran over and gave her a big hug and kiss.

*It's July. It's Florida. In my dark dress, I'm hot. In her white outfit, Stephanie's hot. But Mama still wore her long-sleeved turtleneck and "stir up" pants!*

"Who is that sign for?" she asked me.

"You, Mama!"

"'Welcome Home?'"

"Yes, Mama. This is where you live now."

"Oh, I forgot."

As we started walking through the terminal, I realized I had no idea what floor of the garage I parked on. There are little cards by the parking garage elevators that you can pick up so you know where you parked. I was so excited I forgot to take one. When I told Mom what I did, she laughed.

"Welcome home, Mama. Let our adventures begin," I said.

"You can lose the car, but just don't lose me!"

I took her by the arm. "Don't worry, Mama. It's all going to be great!"

*Happiness is a conscious choice,*
*not an automatic response.*
*Mildred Barthel*

*June 24, 2006*

Our week has been very busy. I took Mama to her new church, ordered her telephone service, picked up her new bed. I took her to see a financial advisor, a dentist, and to get her hair done. We also had lunch each day at Freedom Square Retirement Community. One evening we had dinner with a resident who's on the welcoming committee, although Mama barely spoke.

Mama's apartment is on the fifth floor in the Independence Building at Freedom Square. The place is gorgeous. It's more like a vacation hotel than a senior community. They have independent living, assisted living, and even a nursing home on the campus. But with Mama I doubt we will ever need the nursing home. She and I plan to hang out together for many years to come. I joke with her that when I get older we will have to get a two-bedroom apartment instead of a one-bedroom so she and I can live together.

Her clothes and belongings are on a moving truck but have not yet arrived. Mama seems a bit confused. I am doing a lot of hand-holding with her, just as she has held my hand whenever I needed it. I think once her stuff comes she'll feel more at home.

*June 28, 2006*

Mom's apartment at Freedom Square will not be

ready for her to move into until July 5th! She is perfectly
happy in the guest room at my place. She would stay
with me forever if she could. She has been busy
running around with me every day—as she says, "out
gallivanting."

We will definitely be having breakfast together every
Tuesday, since she has joined the Kiwanis chapter I
belong to. Kiwanis is a global organization of volunteers
dedicated to changing the world one child and one
community at a time. I remember the first couple
of meetings I attended a little over a year ago. I was
instantly struck by the integrity of the group. They
*are* dedicated to making a difference. Everyone was
very welcoming, and had great senses of humor. One
gentleman reminds me of my dad, and I remember
thinking then that I could get into having breakfast
with "my dad" every Tuesday morning. The majority of
members are men and women around Mom's age, give
or take a couple of years, and she loves to volunteer. So
this is perfect for her.

I have been a volunteer since I was a young child.
"Teach your children by example," is one of Mom's
mottoes. Mom was always volunteering for something
at church or our school. From cleaning altar linens to
chaperoning dances to cooking hot dogs at football
games (and she hates hot dogs), Mom did it all. She

always says it doesn't cost you anything to help someone. I recently found a diary of mine from the fifth grade. In it I wrote, "I want to be a volunteer when I grow up." I make a joke that I must have thought volunteering was a paid position. Too bad it isn't—at times I've taken volunteering to the extreme.

Today Mom has volunteered to help out at the Chamber of Commerce. With a couple of other women, she will be stuffing flyers for their monthly newsletter. She knows most of the people from the chamber office, as over the years when she came to visit she helped me with a lot of my own volunteer activities there. They all call her "Mama Jo."

The best part is that I will be dropping her off and someone from the office will drive her home. I need my space. Mom has been very clinging and I have been with her 24/7 since she got here. I understand that everything here is new and a little scary for her, but I just need a little space.

*A faithful friend is the medicine of life.*
*The Apocrypha*

*July 3, 2006*

I am blessed to have a friend like Lin. She has been at Mama's place every day, painting, decorating, organizing, and entertaining Mama. Sometimes she works on Mama's apartment when Mama is not even there. Mama calls Lin "my interior decorator." And Lin has done some terrific job. She just has that special knack for decorating on any budget. When she finishes a room, it always looks like it could be on the cover of *Better Homes & Gardens.*

I have been dragging furniture and all sorts of things to the apartment daily. I am grateful to have a convertible. With the top down, it makes hauling stuff so much easier.

The front desk staff at Freedom Square are getting used to Lin and me trooping through. At first they thought we were sisters but could not understand why we both had the name Linda. Lin told them "our" mom is like George Foreman—she named all her girls Linda. At first I think they thought she was serious, but now they know we're just a bunch of jokers. The tenants seem to love all the spirit we bring to the place. Many of them do not have any visitors. What a pity.

Today, I packed my bag slowly, like a robot. I'll be sleeping at Mom's place until she can get used to being there. Although I am exhausted, I know this is the best thing for her. I want her to feel safe and comfortable. I can totally relate, as I think back to when I first moved here. I didn't know where anything was and my husband and I were in a new house for the first time in twenty-two years. It was a little frightening. But I jumped in, found my way around, and found where I fit in. Now I am looking to carve a space for Mama, to help her fit in and be comfortable.

*July 5, 2006*

As I drove into the parking lot of Seminole City Park today, I could feel the excitement of Mama and my grandkids, Skylar and Tommy. We were there to feed the ducks, blow some bubbles, and ride on the swings.

"Come on, Gramma Jo," Tommy yelled.

*"Gramma Jo" with her great-grandchildren, Skylar and Tommy, shortly after Tommy's birth in 2004.*

"Yes, let's go," Skylar said as she ran toward the lake.

"How cool is this, Mama, coming to the park with your *great*-grandchildren?" I asked.

"On a beautiful day like today and me feeling good, it's good Linda."

When I was a child, not too many kids had great-grandparents. People didn't live as long as they do now.

I am so glad that Mama is here with me. We don't talk a lot about our feelings for each other but we show it in other ways. We are both blessed.

**Dare to be cute.**
*George Lucas*

*July 23, 2006*

A couple of weeks ago I realized the silverware drawer in Mama's kitchen needed repair. When you pulled it out the entire drawer almost fell out of the cabinet. Since Mama is not doing much of anything for herself these days, I wanted her to be the one to call the resident handyman, not me.

"Just call the handyman. You don't have to pay any money, Mama. It's included in your rent."

"I don't know where to call."

"The number is right here on the table where I left it for you two weeks ago."

"I know. I just forget to call."

"Call now, Mama."

"No, I don't feel like it now. I'll call later."

"Promise?"

"Yes, Linda Sue."

Well, lo and behold, today when I went to get a spoon out of Mama's drawer, it was fixed.

"This is great! I'm glad you called, Mama. Now wasn't that easy?"

"Yes, Linda Sue," she said like a smart-aleck kid.

Then this evening when I was leaving Mama's place, she walked me down to the lobby. She does that often and then sits on the bench out by the pond after I leave.

Across the lobby I saw the handyman.

"Thanks so much for fixing my mama's drawer," I yelled.

"It was my pleasure. Any day I can get in your mother's drawers is a good day for me!" he yelled back.

Mama was laughing hysterically.

"I love to get the old coots going," Mama whispered in my ear.

I thought, *Thank you God, Mama has a new story.*

*July 29, 2006*

This afternoon Mama and I were going to the theatre. We both love live shows. I remember years ago when I took Mama and my mother-in-law to see Frank Sinatra. We had second row seats. I had never seen two grown women swoon over a celebrity like they did!

On the way to the show today, Mama said, "These clouds are just so beautiful! So big and fluffy, I just want to grab them."

"Yes, they are wonderful," I agreed. I realized, when you live here for a while and see them every day in the summer, it's easy to stop noticing their shimmering beauty.

"We don't have nice clouds like this in New York. And Linda, when do you stop wearing white around here?" Before I had a chance to answer, she blurted out, "I *hate* that I can't wear my high heels anymore!"

"No, the clouds in New York are definitely not as beautiful. Mama, you can wear white here all year long. And I can barely wear high heels anymore either," I said with a smile.

Mama's routine has always been to wear white shoes and accessories from May through August, and then switch back to black in September. She would also change the curtains and the linens in our house religiously at those times.

One of my fondest memories is when I would return home from visiting my grandma at the end of summer. I'd walk into my bedroom to see it sparklingly beautiful, with a new bedspread and curtains. I still change my curtains and linens according to the season, just like Mama did. One of my friends says it's "an Up North thing." I don't care what it is. I just like it.

*August 9, 2006*

Mama has been telling me how much she misses her car. I don't blame her but I don't know if it is safe for her to drive anymore. During her last year in New York, Mama had to get five or six new tires. She kept hitting curbs and getting blowouts. My brother David would call me and say, "She did it *again!*"

How do you tell your mother she can't drive anymore? How could I tell her I don't trust her judgment driving? If someone told me that, it would piss me off. As far as I am concerned, a car is freedom. I remember when my husband, Tom, and I bought our first house in 1979, in Floral Park, New York. The real estate broker said that for a thirty-year mortgage our payment, including taxes and insurance, would be $687 per month. That was a lot of money then. I remember telling Tom

*The second car Mama ever owned was a 1971 Cadillac. Both she and that car were glamorous!*

I'd give up any extras to get that house—new clothes, entertainment, whatever I had to. But not my car. I had to have my car.

I remember when Mom got her first car. It was only a short time before I got my first one. She loved that car because it gave her more freedom. Her last one was a 1994 Plymouth Sundance. It was a cute little red car and Mama loved it. I made the down payment for it and the four of us chipped in to make the loan payment each month for four years. We wanted Mom to have a brand new car that was safe, so she—and we—wouldn't have to worry about it breaking down or anything. The last couple of years in New York, Mama didn't venture very far with it. Back and forth to church each day or the grocery store. Once a week to Mercy Hospital, to distribute communion as a Roman Catholic Eucharistic minister. And once a week to her sister Margie's in Howard Beach.

For the last couple of weeks, every time Mama got in my car she talked about not having her car.

"Do you want to get a car?" I asked, every time.

"I don't know," Mama said with a shrug of her shoulders.

"Mama, how about we rent a car for a week? You can drive it around and if you feel comfortable with it, then we can go out and look for a car for you."

"You are so smart! That is why I keep you around, Linda Sue."

"I know, Mama."

So we rented a car for a week. By the third day I was still doing all the driving. Each time I asked Mama if she wanted to drive, she would say "Later" or "Tomorrow."

On the fourth day I pulled up in front of Mama's place. When she came out, I was sitting in the passenger seat.

"What are you doing?" Mama asked, almost bewildered.

"Waiting for you to drive me to the bank."

"Tomorrow."

"No, Mama, today. The bank is less than a mile away and we'll take the easiest route."

Mama drove to the bank, white-knuckled all the way. When we got out of the car, she tossed the keys to me and said, "I'm done. I'm not driving anymore."

"Okay, Mama."

*That was simple*, I thought.


*August 20, 2006*

This afternoon I returned from a business convention in Salt Lake City. I was gone for only three days but I feel guilty about having left Mama alone.

I went over to Mama's to have dinner with her in the residents' dining room. When Mama answered her door she greeted me with the enthusiasm of a five-year-old. She told me she had spent most of the time I was gone with my daughter, Nicole. They went shopping, to the movies, played cards, and had dinner together. I love my daughter and love that she loves my mama.

After dinner, Mama gave me a little gift bag. "What's this, Mama?" I asked.

"A back-to-school present," she answered.

I opened the bag and in it found two kitchen towels, a pot holder, and a bag of Hershey kisses. The memories were swirling around in my head. Every year when school started after summer recess, Mama would buy us new back-to-school stuff. And even though we have all been out of school for a long, long time, Mama still gives us little back-to-school gifts. I like this. It makes me smile and I know I will always be Mama's little girl.

I wrapped my arms around her and gave her a big kiss and hug. "Thanks, Mama."

"You're welcome, Lindy Lou."


*September 11, 2006*

I need some *spaaaace*! I've started singing the tune *Me and My Shadow* in my head. Now I understand why so many people name their dogs Shadow.

Mom has really been making the rounds with me. She even has her own 60-second elevator speech for networking meetings. When her turn comes she says, "Hi, my name is Jo McCauley. I just moved here from New York and I am looking for a man with lots of money who just wants to be my friend."

Everyone laughs and some women say things like "Get on line behind me," or "Let me know if he has a twin brother."

She also holds up her crooked, arthritic middle finger (yes, middle finger). She tells a story of some guy cutting her off in traffic and she gets out of her car and yells at him and then gives him the crooked finger and he doesn't know what to do.

They all think it is hysterical but I am just tired of it. If someone else's mom did that, I would think it funny, but not my mom. Is that mean of me? I know I could just not invite her to come to the meetings with me, but then I would feel terribly guilty. I still feel bad for the years Mom spent in New York, retreating more and more into herself in the house (or what I called "the cave"), after I moved to Florida.

Anyway, today I took Mom to another networking breakfast. On the way there I asked her to please not do the crooked finger story. She sighed but said, "Okay."

About an hour into the meeting I heard her telling the finger story to a couple of people at our table. They were laughing but I wanted to slip under the table. Nancy, the gal who sat next to me, said, "My mom has that same crooked finger."

Next I heard Mom telling everyone how she worked for lawyers for years and how none of them had better mess with her.

"My mom worked for lawyers too," Nancy said, smiling. "Your mom reminds me a lot of my mom."

"No way!" We both laughed and decided our moms have to meet each other.

## *Ee-lim-inate the Negative...*

*September 23, 2006*

Today was service Saturday at my church, Unity of Clearwater. Mama came with me to do some volunteer work. It was a delightful morning and Mama truly enjoyed herself.

Mama's memory is really fading, though. When we are driving somewhere she will ask me, over and over again, where we are going. Sometimes I'll get a little flustered and she will say, "I know where we are going. I was just testing you." Well, that's bologna!

I don't want to be flustered. I want to be in the moment with Mama. When she can't remember something or when she keeps repeating the same thing over and over, I want to be patient and remember that the most important thing is not the conversation but that we are together talking.

� ♥ ⱽ⅁

*The ordinary acts we practice every day at home
are of more importance to the soul
than their simplicity might suspect.*
Thomas More

ꚍ ♥ ⱽ⅁

*September 27, 2006*

I took Mama to get her hair done today at the salon
where my daughter Nicole works. Mama is such a
character. She entertains Nicole and everyone else in the
salon. They all love her and look forward to seeing her

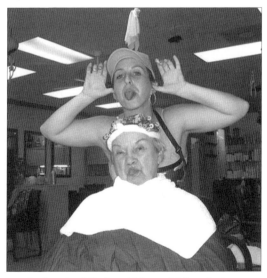

*In the salon, Nicole and Mama didn't need scissors
when it came to cutting up.*

and hearing her stories each week while Nicole makes her beautiful.

After that we went to the movies. Mama has always loved the movies. She tells me that when she was a young girl she could go to the movie theatre for fifteen cents on a Saturday and see three full-length films. For the past couple of years Mama went to the movies by herself in New York. I have vowed to myself that Mama will never go to a movie alone again. One of the best things is the movie theatre is right across the street from where Mama lives. *There are no accidents in life,* I think. We usually go for romantic comedies three or four times a month. And each and every time it is a comedy routine with us.

I walk up to the ticket booth and say, "Two seniors."

Mama stands back with her hand over her mouth giggling. "You're not a senior," she says.

"Yes I am, Mama, this is Florida," I respond.

"Yeah, but you're not that old," she says, giggling more. Then she whispers to me, "What if they ask you for your driver's license?"

"I'll tell them that they took my driver's license away because I'm too old to drive!" We both laugh and laugh as we enter the theatre.

Mama has always said she enjoys going to the movies to escape and be entertained. She doesn't want to see movies with violence or, as she says, movies you have to think about. I agree.

*Plenty of people miss their share of happiness,*
*not because they never found it,*
*but because they didn't stop to enjoy it.*
*William Feather*

*October 10, 2006*

Mama and I went to pick up our new eyeglasses this afternoon. I have this strange thought that maybe she will actually use them, but I doubt it. She laughed hysterically when the optometrist said my eyes are worse than hers. She only really needs them for reading... but she reads nothing these days. As she says, "I have my personal assistant Linda to read for me."

We had a nice dinner in the dining room at Freedom Square. Most of the residents know both of us by name now and they all say hello. Mama says hi back and smiles but she does not know anyone's name. And I don't think it bothers her in the least.

After dinner we went to bingo. Mark my words, this

is the last time I am going with her. They have bingo for the residents every Tuesday and Friday evening. Mama enjoys it. Like all the other residents, Mama sits in the same seat each time. Everyone smiles and chats a little bit but once the bingo games begin, you can hear a pin drop. You are not permitted to have any beverages or snacks and you are not really allowed to talk. If you have any conversation, someone may get distracted and not hear the number that is being called. And this is fun? I think not.

But, Mama enjoys it and she doesn't mind going by herself. So, why do I go with her? Guilt? I don't know but I'm not doing it anymore. No more bingo for me.

Actually, it will be delightful not having to worry about Mama on Tuesday and Friday evenings. Thank God for bingo (tee-hee).

*October 18, 2006*

Mama was supposed to meet me in the lobby of her building, as we were going shopping today. Mama said she needed some odds and ends. When she was not in the lobby waiting for me, I went upstairs and knocked on her door. We have a routine that we have had for many years. I knock on her door, she knows it is me, but she calls out, "Who is it?"

I say, "Linda."

"Linda whoooo?" she sings.

"Linda Su-ue!" I sing back.

She opens the door laughing. I love my Mama.

"Why didn't you meet me downstairs?" I asked.

"I forgot," Mama said, rolling her eyes.

"Let's go!"

"Wait a minute, don't rush me."

"Okay, okay," I said *very* patiently. I watched Mama slowly close the blinds and shut off *Judge Joe Brown* on the television. She just loves those judge shows.

As we got in the car Mama said, "My entire house is clean, all my laundry is done." I thought to myself, *Of course it is—you have a cleaning lady come in once week, you do your three pieces of wash every other day, and I do everything else for you.*

*Be nice, Linda,* I told myself. Like Mama has said since I was a little girl, "If you don't have something nice to say, then don't say anything at all."

Visiting the supermarket with Mama can be quite comical. You would think she had never been in a supermarket before.

"They don't have this in New York. I've never seen this before," she repeats as we walk up and the down the aisles.

I know the store here has everything the stores have in New York, and even more, but I just reply, "Oh, you've just led a sheltered life, Mama. It's good you're here with me now on our adventure."

"I can't believe how many different kinds of jellies they have. I remember when they only had grape and strawberry. This is crazy!" Mama says.

I agree. Too many choices are not always a good thing. We make our lives very complicated. The older I get myself, the more I yearn for a simpler life.

The part she enjoys the most are the free food samples. She stands about ten feet away and says, "Linda, get me some of that."

"You can get it, Mama." I sigh.

"No, I want you to get it for me."

"Okay, Mama."

After the grocery store, we went to Wal-Mart. She needed some things for the house and some new white shoes. We shopped for about two hours. If I were alone, it would have taken me thirty minutes. But I always remind myself, *someday you will be old, Linda, and hopefully someone will be nice enough to take you shopping.*

The only thing she bought was a pair of canvas shoes for five dollars. She is so concerned that she doesn't have enough money. This is the first time in her life she has plenty of money, but she is stuck in her old ways. It kills me that she is walking around with her purse handle safety-pinned together.

Later tonight, I will go back to the store, buy her another pair of shoes, a new purse, and whatever else I think she needs or should have. Then I will bring them to her tomorrow and she will be so excited. She'll ask me, "What do I owe you?"

"Don't worry about it, Mama, we'll figure it out another day," I'll tell her.

We never do figure it out but that doesn't matter. It is my mission for Mama to be comfortable and to have anything she needs or wants. She deserves to be spoiled for once in her life. And I will admit I can be a good spoiler.

***A quiet conscience sleeps in thunder.***
*English proverb*

*October 26, 2006*

Tonight I had a Chamber of Commerce social at my home. It was a huge success. There were probably about seventy people here through the evening, networking and laughing. With a caricature artist and wonderful music by my dear musical-duo friends, Nancy and Steve, a good time was had by all. On top of all this, my brother, David, has flown in for a weekend visit. All night Mama was telling people that she thinks she likes it here—but she hates the heat.

My girlfriend Nancy brought her mom, and the two crooked-finger gals had a wonderful time chatting. My photographer friends Yvonne and Hank took many great photos—including a funny one of the crooked-finger gals.

I drove Mama home later this evening and carried up the groceries we had purchased for her this afternoon. We sat down and chatted a little bit. "I had a fun night tonight," Mama said. "You know a lot of really nice people."

"Mama, I still can't believe you moved here. I heard

*"The crooked finger gals," Elsie and Jo.*

you telling a bunch of people this evening about how much you hate the heat. Why did you decide to move here?"

She looked up and gave me that wonderful smile of hers. "I moved here because, out of all the kids, you make me laugh the most and I know you'll take care of me."

I smiled and thought, *Let me stand on my head so I can make you laugh more, Mama.*

Later, I found myself wondering if she knew then how ill she was.

**Being challenged in life is inevitable.**
**Being defeated is optional.**
Roger Crawford

*October 31, 2006—Halloween*

Mama called me at 6:30 this morning to say that she would not be going to Kiwanis with me because she was not feeling well. This was so not like Mama. She goes everywhere with me. I asked if she wanted me to come over but she told me to go to the meeting and then come. After the meeting, when I knocked at her front door, she didn't greet me with our usual routine. When I walked in, she looked terrible—or, as Mom would say, "like death warmed over."

She was very weak. My first thought was to make her some tea. Then the light bulb went off in my head—Mama lives in Freedom Square, we have help here. I called down to the main desk and told them, "Mama is not feeling well. Could you please send a nurse up to check her out?"

"Linda, I don't need a nurse," Mama insisted.

"Maybe not, Mama, but better safe than sorry. Remember, I'm not the nurse daughter. That's Patty." I made a goofy face and Mom laughed.

Within a few minutes the resident nurse came up. While she took Mama's temperature and checked her vitals, Mama was making jokes and funny faces.

"Linda, you need to get her to the hospital right away," the nurse said.

"Right away?"

"Yes. Immediately."

I took Mama over to the emergency room at Largo Medical Hospital. She didn't want to go but she was too weak to argue with me. We spent the entire day there while they ran all sorts of tests. Mom needed four blood transfusions.

I joked, "Mama, it's Halloween, we didn't need to come to the hospital for blood. We could have gotten you some from a vampire."

Mama only smiled weakly.

I still have no idea what is wrong. Mom kept saying that she was fine and wanted to go home. They didn't tell me much except that she was going to be admitted. I was really worried but I tried to keep things light. I wished my sister Pat was here. I hate this hospital stuff.

At 10 P.M., I thought I could go home. "Can't you stay?" Mama asked.

I wanted to scream! I was tired and I had a right to be tired, but that didn't give me the right to be crabby. I feel like I've become the mother now and part of it terrifies me.

"I have to go home Mama. We both need to sleep. I'll be back early in the morning. I love you."

"I love you too. Good night and God bless, Linda."

I realize clearly now how listening is an act of love.

*Fear is a reaction. Courage is a decision.*
*Winston Churchill*

*November 1, 2006*

Mom has cancer!

Cancer. *Cancer!!!*

That's impossible.

It's colon cancer. They want to do surgery tomorrow. The words float in and out of my head. I feel like I am going to pass out. Pat has been communicating with the doctors, thank God. As a nurse, she can understand what they're telling her and translate it for the rest of us.

How can this be? How can Mom be sick? She just got here! She is comfortable here now and she is truly enjoying herself.

This sucks. My mama is not supposed to have cancer. The 'C' word scares the hell out of me.


*November 2, 2006*

The hospital is quiet. Sitting here next to her bed, I occasionally hear someone talking softly or the sound of one of the machines that seem to be attached to every patient for some reason or another.

Mama is out like a light. When I saw the size of her incision I felt weak. I feel so frustrated because there is nothing I can do for her. I wonder how many times Mama felt frustrated when I was hurting emotionally or physically and there was nothing she could do for me.

Ever since I was born, Mama has demonstrated love

that is complete and unconditional. I want her to feel confident that I am here for her no matter what.

Mama and I have decided that life is a playground, not a laboratory, and we're staying on the merry-go-round.

*November 5, 2006*

Mom is still in the hospital. Did I say her incision is huge? She's out of it most of the time. I am at my wit's end. Between my husband's case of the shingles and Mama, I am running back and forth, taking care of both of them. There's not much to do for Tom, as he just sits in the recliner all day watching TV, but I feel guilty that I'm not home much to take care of him.

And trying to run my businesses—well, that is just a joke! I'd need another ten hours in a day.

In Mama's hospital room today, I felt so stressed. Then a little voice in my head said, *Sit down, Linda, and breathe.* I sat down, took a drink of water, closed my eyes, and said a little prayer. I don't know how long I sat there, but when I opened my eyes a nurse was standing in front of me. "Are you okay?" she asked.

"Yes, I'm fine. Just a little tired."

"Your mother had a very peaceful night last night. She seems to be getting a bit stronger."

"I am so glad. I just want to get her home."

"Go home and get some rest for yourself, so you'll be able to take care of her when she does come home," the nurse said kindly.

"I want to wait until she wakes up, so she knows I was here."

About a half hour later Mom woke up.

"Are you hungry, Mama?" I asked.

"No, I'm sick of this crap. Get me out of here, Linda."

"All in due time, Mama. We have to get you out of ICU first."

Mama looked at me with her sad, bloodshot eyes. I brushed her hair and cleaned her up a little. I showed her some cards the kids had made for her. And then I started entertaining Mama, as I always do, cracking jokes and just being silly. Mama laughed and laughed.

I told her that I had to go but would be back later.

"Thank you honey. I love you," Mama said with a warm smile on her face.

"You don't have to thank me for anything, Mama. I love you too."

I gave her a kiss and left. As I walked down the hallway to the elevator the tears started to flow. And I realized that, no matter how far I go or how much I achieve, few accomplishments in my life are as rewarding as a single smile from my mother's heart. The gratitude that flows from my heart is the mortar that holds all in place.

**Two are better than one ... if one falls down,
his friend can help him up.**
*Ecclesiastes 4:9-10*

*November 12, 2006*

You can tell Mama is getting stronger. She is out of ICU and she's getting feisty. When the doctor asked her today how she was doing, she said, "Fine" and stuck her tongue out like a wise guy.

Thank you, God. As soon as she stuck her tongue out I knew she was getting back to normal.

*November 14, 2006*

Mama was released from the hospital today. A home health care service will be checking on her daily. Thank God, because I am feeling really nervous. I can't even look at her incision without feeling faint—never mind trying to change her bandages. I guess I could if I had to, but I don't want to.

And Mama's meds are always changing. I can barely keep track of them and she sure can't. Sometimes they give her a generic and it is a different color than the previous one she was taking. And some of them look exactly the same. It can be very confusing.

It is going to take a while, but we will get through this together. We are going to beat this stinking cancer!

As I consider my experiences in life, I have a choice: I can focus on the happy experiences and the successes, or I can focus on the sad and disappointing ones.

Then I realize there might be a better choice—to embrace all experiences for whatever value I have gained from them.

*November 29, 2006*

Mama was sitting in my den watching television while I did a little paperwork in the office.

"Is there anything I can do to help you?" Mama called out to me.

"No, Mama, I'm fine."

About thirty minutes later I found Mama napping in front of the TV. Mama has never been a napper. This is just another reminder that Mama is older. In my mind I still see her as thirty years old.

I went back into my office and a little bit later Mama called out, "Do you have some cheese and crackers?"

"Sure, Mama, let me get you some. Did you have a nice nap?"

"I wasn't napping."

"Yes you were."

"I was just resting my eyes."

"Sure, Mama. Here's your cheese and crackers."

"How about a cold beer too?" she asked.

"No problem, Mama." One of her favorite things has always been a cold beer and pretzels, and she deserves whatever she wants.

I went back into my office to finish up. When I walked back into the den, Mama was staring at her hands with a frown.

"Are you okay, Mama?"

"I'm fine. Just looking at these old ugly hands. They sure are a mess."

"Oh Mama, they're not so bad. In fact, I think those hands are pretty fantastic. Besides, as you often remind me, they have washed a lot of clothes and scrubbed a lot of floors. But they also have washed my face, tied my shoes, and combed my hair. Those hands have held my baby daughter and also my grandchildren. Those hands have wiped away my tears and also given me a whack on the behind when I needed it. Think about it Mama—those hands have done a lot."

"I guess they have," Mama said with a smile.

"Let me put the crock-pot on for dinner and then let's go for a pedicure and manicure and treat those beautiful hands."

"That sounds good," Mama said with a big smile on her face.

*Attention is the most basic form of love;*
*through it we bless and are blessed.*
John Tarrant

*December 10, 2006*

We sent out Mama's Christmas cards this morning. There is a picture of Jesus on the front and inside it says, "You are truly blessed. Merry Christmas." She also included the following note: "Christmas time is different in Florida with all the warm weather and the palm trees but I am thoroughly enjoying myself. I miss you all and can't wait until you come and visit. Please keep me in your prayers when I start my chemo in January. With love, Jo."

I still don't want to believe that she has cancer.

Tonight Mama wanted to go to the beach to see the sunset. She said she has never been to the beach in December and she wanted to go. She was all decked out in her usual uniform—turtleneck, sweatshirt, and stirrup pants, but hey, we were going to the beach. I packed us a couple of sandwiches, and a jelly donut for Mom. Grabbed a couple of beach chairs and some sunglasses for Mama and off we went. It was a lovely evening.

"This is just beautiful," Mama said.

"Aren't you glad you live in paradise?" I asked.

"It's okay," Mama said, looking at me out of the corner of her eye with a little smirk on her face.

"Admit it, Mama. You love it."

"It's okay."

"If you don't admit it, no jelly donut!" I said laughing.

"I love it, I love it, I love it!" Mama said through her laughter.

I gave her the jelly donut and she ate it as we sat in silence, enjoying the sunset and being with each other. Sitting there together I just felt so grateful for sunrises and sunsets. The apparent changes in each, morning and night, encourage me and remind me that each day is a new day in my life.

ବ ♥ ଛ

**You don't get to choose how you're going to die.
Or when. You can only decide
how you're going to live, now.**
*Joan Baez*

ବ ♥ ଛ

*December 18, 2006*

Mama had a port put into the left side of her chest today. This is so when she starts her chemo, they won't have to be poking holes into her each time. They will just plug the chemo "cocktail" into her port.

"Those clouds are beautiful," Mama said as we drove to the hospital. "Thank you for taking me, Linda. I know you have much work to do."

"Nothing is more important than you, Mama."

I feel so overwhelmed. I called my sister Stephanie last night. I think she thinks that I am in denial. If I *was* in denial, I wouldn't be so upset.

"You knew Mama was going to die someday," she said.

I was so angry. "Yes, I know she is going to die someday. Just not so soon!" I cried.

While we were sitting in the hospital after her

procedure, out of the blue Mama said to me, "May you know one of my greatest blessings was having you!"

"Thank you, Mama," I whispered.

I pray that my actions are always ones that benefit my mama.

## *All I Want for Christmas...*

*December 20, 2006*

Mama left for New York this afternoon. I'm not really that happy about it but I hope I'll have her in Florida for many more Christmases. I know that even though it hasn't been long since she moved, my siblings really miss Mama. I'm glad that the four of us get along so well. We've disagreed with each other, even disappointed one another, but we accepted those times, knowing they would pass and we'd all come to understand again how each of us really loves one another.

Christmas is Mama's favorite holiday. When I was a child she would start her shopping in August. She would come home with a mischievous look on her face and declare, "I bought you a gift for Christmas today!" Then she would giggle and run upstairs to hide it. Christmas morning in our house on Spruce Street was where children's dreams came true. The house was always beautifully decorated, inside and out. Mama always insisted that the lights on the outside of the house were to be blue only. String those lights up on that English Tudor and on the big trees on each side of the front porch, add a little snow, and the McCauley home looked like something on a Thomas Kinkaid card. Just lovely.

I know she'll be glad to go to midnight Mass at St. Thomas. And she will be back on December 30 so we will be able to celebrate New Year's together.

*December 24, 2006*

Mama has been in the hospital in New York. She had a bowel obstruction. I feel like I should have seen something. She has gone through a lot the past two months and, although looking tired, Mama's insists she feels fine. I'm doubting myself. Am I doing right by my mama?

Pat has let me know that she feels I'm not doing such a great job. But I'm not a nurse. I don't know what to look for. When you see someone every day, changes are so subtle. I try to make sure Mama eats right and that she gets enough rest. I make sure she takes her medications and vitamins, and I take Mama to all her doctor appointments religiously. And each and every time the doctor asks, "How are you doing, Mrs. McCauley?" she says, "Fine."

"Is anything bothering you?" the doctor asks.

"No, I'm fine," Mama says.

Then, if I know she has been complaining about gas or diarrhea or tiredness or a pain or whatever, I jump in and tell the doctor about it. Then Mama says, "Oh yeah."

I am doing the best I can.

*Okay, enough Linda, stop the whining.*

**A heart is not judged by how much you love,**
**but by how much you are loved by others.**
—*The Wizard of Oz to the Tin Man*

*December 26, 2006*

Mama was released from the hospital on Christmas Eve. Naturally, the first thing she wanted to do was get her hair done. Pat took her and then that evening they went to Mass. Christmas Day everyone in the family surrounded Mama—Pat and her husband, Wayne, and her son Robert; Wayne's children and grandchildren; Stephanie and her boyfriend, Chip; David and his wife, Kathy. Although still not feeling well, it was a lovely day Mama told me.

*December 28, 2006*

Mama left Pat's on the 26<sup>th</sup> and traveled to
Pennsylvania with Stephanie and Chip. Although this
was their original plan, Mama was weak and feeling
sick. Stephanie said she wasn't comfortable with Mama
making the trip to Pennsylvania, since the ride would be
nearly five hours from Long Island even without traffic.
But Mama wanted to go and Pat was persistent that she
should.

Stephanie said throughout the trip Mama did her
usual singing, tapping, humming, and so on. Stephanie
also noted that it's funny how that habit of Mama's—
which at times makes us all a little nutty—became music
to her ears, knowing that someday she would never hear
it again.

Chip dropped off Mama and Stephanie at Steph's
place in York and then went home to his farm in New
Oxford. The next day both Mama and Steph came down
with a stomach virus. They said they didn't know which
end to put on the potty first. Although they were both
couch potatoes all that day and night, Stephanie was glad
to be with Mama.

That evening Chip announced that he had a surprise
for the next day. He told them he wanted Mama to get
a good feel for what Pennsylvania was really all about.
He would pick up the two of them before sunrise in the

morning. He told them to dress casual but warmly.

"I hope he doesn't think I'm going to milk a cow or something," Mama muttered to Steph.

Stephanie said she wasn't up for surprises but Chip seemed so excited, almost animated, that she and Mama both agreed.

The next day Chip picked them up and they all arrived at his place just as the sun was about to rise. Even though it was relatively warm for December, Chip felt that Mama wasn't dressed appropriately for his plan, so he suited her up in one of his bright orange hunting jackets and put a wide, warm headband on her head.

Mama laughed. "Don't mess up my coif!"

"You look great, Mama Jo," Chip told her.

"Yeah sure, we look like two refugees from the bo-bo patch," Mama replied. That has always been one of Mama's favorite expressions.

"Like I said before, you look great, Mama Jo," Chip said. "Now, I'm going to run ahead and my sister Lois will be by shortly to pick you both up."

Just minutes later Lois appeared and drove Mama and Steph to a nearby farm. They could see Chip up on a hill. He was leaning back and appeared to be pulling on a rope. They couldn't see what was on the other end of the rope because there was a big barn in the way. He motioned for them to come up the hill.

To their surprise, at the top of the hill there was a huge hot air balloon with a sign on it that read, "Stephanie, will you marry me?"

Stephanie was dumbfounded and Mama was just utterly delighted.

Then the pilot fired up the balloon as Mama and Steph shrieked and laughed. Chip said later that he told Mama he was going to carry her closer to heaven than she had ever been!

Up, up, and away they went, gently floating over pastures and streams. What a peaceful means of transportation. Mama was filled with joy!

As it turned out, a hot air balloon cannot just land anywhere. Within a half hour the balloon pilot started

*Mama was thrilled with the ride of her life, even though the balloon landing provided more adventure than expected.*

hollering down to a farmer, asking if it would be okay to land in his field. Mama and Steph were freaked! Mama mumbled, "I hope the farmer doesn't have a shotgun!"

They landed in the middle of a cornfield. But unlike the balloon in *The Wizard of Oz*, this balloon basket did not have a door, so when they landed Mama couldn't get out. The guys, in their infinite male wisdom, decided to detach the balloon and turn the basket sideways to get Mama out. What were they thinking?! This was December. Mom had major surgery in November. Her stomach and leg muscles are not strong. Once they tipped the basket sideways, she did not have the ability to get up on her own. She was all rolled up in the bottom of the basket with this huge orange hunting jacket scrunched up around her ears. She had to be embarrassed and uncomfortable. But Mama just laughed and laughed. God bless her. What a sport!

Once they got her out of the basket, the pilot broke out the bubbly and Chip, on bended knee, asked Stephanie to be his wife.

"Yes, yes!" Stephanie gushed. Later she told me it was then that she understood why Pat insisted Mama should go to Pennsylvania, even though she was so sick.

Mama was simply delighted. And still is. For the first time, all her children have partners to share their lives with. That is really important to Mama.

*You are younger today than you will ever be again.
Make use of it for the sake of tomorrow.*
Norman Cousins

*January 2, 2007*

*Chemotherapy—definition, from the free encyclopedia Wikipedia:
"Chemotherapy, in its most general sense, refers to treatment
of disease by chemicals that kill cells, specifically those of
micro-organisms or cancer. In popular usage, it usually refers to
antineoplastic drugs used to treat cancer or the combination of these
drugs into a standardized treatment regimen."*

I can feel Mama's nervousness about starting chemo
tomorrow. Neither of us really understand it. We just
know it's supposed to suppress the cancer, and that it
can make you feel sick and tired. I am nervous and I'm
just the chauffeur!

We are definitely not adept at expressing our feelings
verbally but we both know how strong our love is for
each other. I have spent most of my life expressing the
most personal things in my life with a pen and paper, so
today I gave her the following letter:

*Dear Mama,*

*Tomorrow is your first day of chemo. I know you are a little nervous as I am also. I just want you to know how much I love you. I will always take care of you. I will always be here for you as you have always been there for me. We are in this fight together. I will do anything I can to make you feel comfortable, both physically and mentally. I am so grateful for you. And I am grateful we are on this journey together.*

*With all my love, Linda*


*January 3, 2007*

Mama started chemo today—about five hours worth—then there's another round tomorrow and then back on the fifth to have the pump disconnected.

When I picked her up this morning she asked me, "Where are we going?"

Where are we going? Where are we going? I wanted to scream, *"We're going for freakin' chemo, Mama! Freakin' chemo!"* I felt like I was going to be sick. I closed my eyes for a moment as we stopped at a traffic signal. I breathed deeply and said softly, "Mama, your chemo begins today."

"I guess we have to try it," she said ever so softly.

"I guess so," I said.

It all felt so strange. Mama was very quiet as I assured

her that I was there for her then and that I would be the entire time.

"I will not leave you, Mama."

"Promise?" she asked, looking at me with sad eyes.

"Yes, Mama, I promise."

"You better promise or I'll have to give you a wung-tung," Mama said with a little smile on her face.

Mama has been telling us she would give us a "wung-tung" since we were kids. None of us is still quite sure what a "wung-tung" is, but I don't want one.

My eyes scanned the waiting room. Everyone was like a blur to me. I wondered what kinds of cancer they have, how long they have had it, and if they will beat it. My heart was heavy. As I made eye contact with some of the people I gave them a big smile. Each one returned it, but none of the smiles lasted long. Many looked just exhausted. Some read and many just sat and stared. A woman walked in—she was completely bald. Mama cringed and squeezed my arm.

I gave Mama a hug as the nurse called out, "Josephine McCauley."

We walked into a long room. Very sterile. One side of the room was lined with mini recliners, about twenty of them in all. On the opposite wall, up high, there were about six different televisions—each with a different channel on, of course. The staff was all cheerful and they wore brightly colored scrubs.

*Yeah, this is cheery,* I thought angrily.

The nurse took Mama's temperature, blood pressure, and a little blood from her finger. Just watching them prick her finger I felt faint. Even the Band-Aids were cheerfully bright colors. The nurse then told Mama that in the future she should not wear a turtleneck, as it makes it harder for them to hook into the port. *Good luck,* I thought. Mama without a turtleneck. I can't imagine it. When the nurse turned her back, Mama stuck out her tongue.

Yes, this is going to be an adventure. Mama made a funny face at me. I made one back at her and we both laughed. *Bring it on,* I thought to myself.

I made sure that Mama was comfortable. She said she was going to read *The Enquirer,* but I doubted it. She barely reads anything these days.

Reminds me of the time she and I went to Ireland three years ago. Every time we would go into a restaurant, Mama would want me to read the menu to her.

"Mama, don't you have your eyeglasses with you?" I asked.

"They're in my suitcase."

"You need to bring them with you, Mama."

"No I don't, you can read for me."

"What?"

"I decided last year that since I've worked hard my entire life, I don't have to do anything I don't feel like doing, so you can read for me, Linda Sue."

And being the good daughter, that is what I did. Until the last night we were there … I was a nervous wreck the whole time we were in Ireland, what with driving on the opposite side of the car and the road, the roundabouts, and Mama not helping me with maps or signs or anything. I made sure I did not drink any alcohol while we were there. Then on the last night we went to dinner at a castle. They gave us some drink that had alcohol in it, although I didn't realize it at the time. After my second or third goblet I started to feel it. I was a little nervous about driving back to the bed-and-breakfast but thought it would be okay since I only had one road to take for about a half a mile. Well, it was very dark and I must have driven back and forth past that place about six times. I pulled the car over to the side of the road and wanted to choke my mother.

"Mama, do you want to sleep in this car tonight?" I yelled.

"No, Linda."

"Then put your glasses on and *help me*!!"

Mama put her glasses on and the next thing I remember was waking up the following morning. My head was splitting. Mama was all dressed, sitting on the edge of her neatly made bed.

"I'm sorry if I yelled at you last night, Mama."

"Oh, that's okay," she said with a big smile. "Now get up and get dressed. I'm hungry."

"Okay Mama."

I am searching for the sacred in the ordinary, with gratitude in my heart, and I think I have found it.

***Our greatest weakness lies in giving up.***
*Thomas Alva Edison*

*January 17, 2007*

Chemo, round two.

Right now my emotions are like a cyclone. Much of my life I have gone to great lengths to avoid them but now I cannot deny them. They are joyful and very painful at the same time. There is an unbearable ache in my heart. But then I am also grateful to have that ache because I love Mama so much.

Does that make sense? Whether it does or not, that's the way it is.

*January 20, 2007*

Mama has been just so sick from the chemo. I have never seen her like this. She just lies on the couch. In my fifty-three years, I have never seen her lie on a couch. The only time Mama ever lays down is when it is time for bed. And the other day she said to me, "Linda, if your smiling face is the last thing I see in my life…"

*No Mama, no! Don't talk like that*, screamed in my head.

We made a family decision to stop the chemo. This is no quality of life for Mama. This is not living.

No matter how prepared we are for the inevitable, attending to a parent's care is always distressing and difficult for mid-life women, turning us into caregivers again at the very time those days were meant to be over, and stretching our schedules as well as our sanity to the breaking point.

**People who never get carried away should be.**
*Malcolm Forbes*

*February 22, 2007*

We are on a cruise—yippee! It is a networking cruise, actually. Funny, Mama has done so much networking with me that she calls me the "Networking Queen" and herself the "Networking Princess." We departed Tampa today. We will sail to Cozumel and back. Five days and four nights of fun are ahead of us. Originally it was to be Mom, Nicole, and me, but Pat and our cousin Natalie decided to join us. Today is Pat's fiftieth birthday. Mama says Pat and I being over fifty makes her feel old.

I will be working part of the cruise but that is great, as it gives Nicole some alone time with Mom. Although Mama sees her granddaughter once a week when Nicole does her hair, and occasionally when Nicole has her over for dinner, they don't get too much time alone. Mama sees her great-grandchildren, Skylar and Tommy, much more often than she sees their mom.

Nicole, Mama, and I are sharing a room, and Pat and Natalie have their own rooms. It is the perfect arrangement for all of us. One of the best parts of the cruise is all the pictures the photographers take. And I sure will take advantage of all opportunities.

On the deck, as the ocean mists my face and the wind gently rustles my hair, I cherish and am so grateful for this time with my family.

*February 24, 2007*

Mama and Nicole each won more than a hundred dollars on the ship's nickel slot machines. The two of them are so excited they can't stop giggling. I'm glad they had fun together, because I can tolerate the slots but really prefer not to. Seeing the smiles on Nicole's and Mama's faces just warmed my heart. This is a trip we will never forget.

**Laughter is an instant vacation.**
*Milton Berle*

*March 8, 2007*

We got some great photos on the cruise. One was taken on the last evening. Mama was dressed up in an old-fashioned dress and she had a big rifle in her hands and a mean scowl on her face. Above the photo it said "WANTED," and underneath it said "$100,000 REWARD." Mama and I decided to have a little fun with it, so we downloaded the photo onto the front of a greeting card and sent one to everyone up north. Inside the card it said:

"*Dear_____,*

*Got in a little trouble in Mexico. Please pray for me!*
*Love, Jo*"

We never laughed so hard! Mama said she almost wet her pants.

I am so glad that we can laugh so easily. Psychologists say the ability to appreciate humor and the ability to laugh actually has physiological effects on the body that cause people to become more bonded.

*March 10, 2007*

Today was the Kiwanis pancake fundraiser. I thought it might be too much for Mama but she still wants to go everywhere with me. We were there at 6 A.M. with our aprons on. She cracks me up. She spent most of the time telling me what I should be doing. And the rest of the time she was telling different people all sorts of stories about me as a child. There are no secrets with Mama around, and everyone so enjoys chatting with her. If it makes her happy, that works for me.

*March 14, 2007*

I could scream! Why doesn't she listen to me? The plan for today was for me to pick Mama up this afternoon and take both of us to vote and then have dinner together.

The best laid plans of mice and women...

As I was trying to catch up on some of my work this morning, someone from Freedom Square called to tell me Mama had fallen down and got hurt. I rushed over there and found Mama with a huge gash in her leg. She had forgotten I was going to take her to vote so she went to the precinct with her neighbors on the Freedom Square bus. Walking across the parking lot at the polling place, she tripped and fell onto a tree stump.

Her skin is just so tender and raw. It looks so painful.

"I'm sorry, Linda," was all she said.

Why doesn't she listen to me?

*Because she forgets, Linda. Because she forgets.*

# The Party Crew

*One's philosophy is not best expressed in words; it is
expressed in the choices one makes. In the long run,
we shape our lives and we shape ourselves. The process
never ends until we die. And, the choices we make are
ultimately our own responsibility.*
Eleanor Roosevelt

*March 20, 2007*

When the alarm clock rings I push the snooze button
and pull the covers over my head. *Please let me sleep just a
little bit longer.*

Today Mama had a check-up with the doctor at
Freedom Square. I knew I needed to get up and get her
moving or she'd just forget about the appointment. I

called Mama to make sure she was up. "Good morning Sunshine, hello World!" she sang into the phone.

I'm glad she has some energy because mine is depleted. We just returned from five days in New York and Pennsylvania—or Pennsyltucky, as we now so fondly call it. We had planned a surprise wedding shower for Stephanie and even a major snowstorm did not stop us from getting there. Thank God for Pat. She is such a trooper. Nothing keeps her down. If she'd had to get a snowplow she would have, to make sure we pulled off the shower.

The snow was so bad we postponed the shower from Saturday to Sunday. We were doubtful if anyone would make it except the people who lived in Pennsylvania, which was mostly Chip's family. The shower was held at Chip's sister's house. Pat and I were bringing all the food, decorations, favors, and so on. Pat, Mama, and I arrived about an hour or so before the party and proceeded to set everything up, then after the shower we cleaned up and drove back home to New York.

The best part was the look on Stephanie's face when she walked in and saw Mama. She was absolutely shocked and cried like a baby.

We McCauley girls definitely stick together and try to never disappoint one another. Mama taught us well.

❧ ♥ ❧

*There are only two lasting bequests we can give our children. One is roots, the other is wings.*
Hodding Carter II

❧ ♥ ❧

*April 11, 2007*

Stephanie and Chip's wedding in Lancaster, Pennsylvania is in three days. Tom and I are driving but that would be too much for Mama, so she flew to New York this evening and will ride up to the wedding with Pat and Wayne.

I'm glad Mama will have some time alone with Wayne and Pat. And I am glad that I will have time alone with my husband. Tom has been very understanding with everything that's going on, and I am grateful.

Originally Stephanie and Chip were going to get married sometime six to twelve months from now. But, with the health conditions of both Mama and Daddy, they decided to move it up. It's good that Stephanie followed her intuition.

*April 14, 2007*

Stephanie and Chip's wedding was perfectly lovely.

*The McCauley Clan: David, Mama, Daddy, Stephanie, me and Pat*

Mama and Daddy were both feeling good and had a wonderful time. Mama was delighted. For the first time in a long time, Mama knew that all of her children were with partners they truly loved and were happy.

Most of our relatives were there and very glad to see Mama. They all say how wonderful Mama looks. They say, "She *can't* be sick!"

*Maybe we're beating it,* I think. *Maybe we're beating it.*


*May 3, 2007*

Today I received an e-mail from a friend of mine, Paula. We met a few years ago through a women's networking organization that I started. I have always liked her and I would describe her as honest, refreshing, and sincere. I called her, as we hadn't spoken in quite some time. I told her that Mama now lived in Florida. She remembered meeting Mama several years ago and reminded me I always said I was going to have Mama's stories recorded. That's what she does—helps people and families capture their life stories as legacies for the future. I know I had thought about doing this before. I decided now was the time to get going.

I went to Mama's this afternoon and told her that I am going to have a friend come and interview her about her life.

"Why would someone want to do that?" Mama asked.

"For the fun of it!" I answered.

"Okay."

Mama's first interview is set for June 1st.


*June 13–18, 2007*

We are off to Michigan! I don't know when Mama was in Michigan last but I think it was probably about fifteen years ago. My dad's older sister, Aunt Kay, and most of her children and their families live there. Even though Mom and Dad have been divorced for many years, Mama has still remained close with Dad's family.

Last month I suggested to Mama that we go for a visit and she was all up for it. One of the wonderful things about Mom is that she will go just about anywhere or do just about anything I suggest. I love Michigan. It is so much less busy and more laid back compared to New York or even Florida. Whenever I think of Michigan, I think of nature.

Most of our time was spent talking, laughing, eating, and playing games. It was just delightful and a definite escape from reality. My cousin said she had never in her life seen Mama so relaxed and at peace. That gave me a wonderful feeling and some optimism.

*I trust in you, O Lord. You are my God.*
*My days are in your hand...*
*Psalm 31:14-15*

*July 17, 2007*

Today Stephanie and I took Mama to see the oncologist. After our usual joking around, Dr. H told us the cancer has spread to her liver. Her CEA level was 21.9 in January and 11.9 in February, which was much

better, but now it is 177.0 I don't fully understand these
blood test results, but I know it is not good. I wish Pat
were here. Bottom line: if Mom chooses not to do more
chemo, then she most likely will have only about six
months to live.

When the doctor said those words, the three of us
sort of went numb. We all heard it loud and clear but
no one said a thing. We left the hospital and went out to
lunch.

Six months—180 *days*! That can't be possible. I
thought Mom was doing so well. I can't believe it! I don't
*want* to believe it. She looks good. She says she feels
good. This is not fair!!!

What do I do now?

The answers come very quickly—

    a. Take care of Mom and keep her as comfortable
       as possible

    b. Keep Mom laughing everyday—and believe
       me, that is not difficult

    c. Read as much as I can to learn about what is
       happening

    d. Spend more time with Mom every day

    e. Pray

I have only really learned to pray in the past
seven years, since I started attending Unity Church in
Clearwater. I was brought up Roman Catholic—I went

to Catholic grammar school and high school, I was part
of the guitar Mass, the teen club, and I even worked at
the rectory. But I felt fearful in my religion. That if I did
*this* or didn't do *that* I would go to hell. At Unity Church
I am taught of love, of possibilities, and of God's
unconditional love for me. And here I have truly learned
to pray and honor the Lord.

*July 24, 2007*

Stephanie went home yesterday. I feel depressed but
I know keeping a good outlook is the only thing that will
get us through this.

The whole world changes when you are told your
mother is going to die. Of course, I knew she would
die someday, but not so soon. Mama loves living here
and she has really settled in, to a point where she is truly
enjoying her life.

I can be a control freak at times and now the lack of
power to control this makes me have to let go.

I have been trying so hard not to know this, but the
truth keeps insisting itself on me.

*August 7, 2007*

Picked up Mama at Tampa International Airport this
afternoon. She loved spending time with Pat and Wayne.
It's so easy when she flies into Islip, Long Island—it's

a small airport very close to Pat's house. The happiness of her children is very important to Mama. Always has been, always will be.

Mama loves Wayne or, as she calls him, "W." When Mama lived in New York she would always bring jelly donuts for Wayne when she went to visit.

She had a busy visit! Pat took her to visit our "aunt," Sister Helen, at the convent. Then David picked her up and took her to visit her dear friend, Olive. Another day, Pat invited four of Mama's friends from St. Thomas for lunch. Each person who visited with Mama would say, "Are you sure she is ill? She looks just wonderful."

One day Daddy and his wife, Heidi, and all of the family on Mama's side came for dinner. How cool is that??

Since Mama moved to Florida, she is not always thinking clearly. Sometimes she knows her house in West Hempstead has been sold and at other times I hear her tell people it has not. I suggested to Stephanie that she take Mama to West Hempstead so Mama could see that the house is sold.

Well, she did. When I picked Mama up from the airport, she told me the story.

"Stephanie took me to Spruce Street. The house has been sold. I can't believe they cut down all my bushes out front. Stephanie and I went to the back yard and I hiked her up on my shoulders."

*Yeah sure*, I thought.

"When we looked in the window I saw that they ripped out my beautiful countertop and cabinets."

*Those cabinets and yellow countertop were thirty years old!* I thought. *They* needed *ripping out!*

"And you're not going to believe it, Linda, but when we were leaving, the garage door opened slowly and there was a *man* in there and he had a mattress in there! Stephanie and I went to the neighbors' and they said a homeless man has been living in the garage!"

I laughed. "Be honest, Mama. That was your boyfriend. You never told him that you were moving and he has been looking for you!"

Mama laughed and laughed. "You are crazy, Linda Sue."

*Yeah, crazy about you*, I thought.

**Happiness is when what you think,
what you say, and what you do
are in harmony.**
*Mahatma Ghandi*

*August 21, 2007*

I just love having my own greeting card business. I've been going through some of Mom's old photos, to put on cards. Everyone has said I should go through the pictures now, because in the end I will be too sad or distracted for a long time. Most of the photos are in albums that I set up for Mom right before I moved to Florida.

I found a photograph recently of Mom with her sisters Lee and Margie, and another woman. They looked to be in their late teens or early twenties. They were all giggling and looked so carefree. I put the photo on the front of a greeting card and sent one to Mama and one

*Aunt Lee, Mama, Aunt Margie, and Who???*

to Aunt Lee. Inside, I just wrote, "Those were the days."

When Mom got her card she called. "Who is that other woman with me and Lee and Margie?"

"I don't have a clue, Mama. Maybe you should call Aunt Lee. She might remember."

The next day I came home to find a message on my answering machine from Aunt Lee. In her Brooklyn accent she said, "Linda Sue, I love these cards you send me. But don't send me a card with someone on it that I do not know! I was up all night trying to figure out who it was!"

I have been sending cards to everyone in the family as I come across great photos. Last week I sent all my cousins on Mom's side a card with a wonderful photo of Mom's parents, Grandma and Grandpa Dean, on the front.

I came across another photo of Mom and Aunt Jean from around 1950. Two good-looking broads, as my dad would say. I sent them each a card. I was with Mama when she got hers in the mail.

She opened the envelope and stared at the photo with a really funny look on her face. "I think I have the same shirt on," she blurted out.

Oh my goodness, I couldn't believe it. Not the exact same shirt, but darn close! I guess Mom's taste in clothes hasn't changed much. We laughed so hard we cried.

Although we are having fun, my heart is breaking.
I always want to do what is best. And quiet moments
in communion with God help me know what to do for
Mama.

*August 22, 2007*

Today I took Mama to Sam's Club with me to do a
little shopping. She loves the Danish and muffins they
have there.

I stood and observed Mama as she picked up one
box of muffins, put it down gently, then picked up
another, looked it over, and put it down. She then said to
me, as she does just about every single time we are there,
"Can you freeze these, Linda? The price is so good but I
could never eat all of these by myself."

"Yes, Mama, you can freeze them," I said as I rolled
my eyes. It's funny, she usually buys them but I have
never seen any in her freezer.

Mama continued to inspect all the boxes of Danish
until she found just the right one and then handed it to
me with a smile on her face. I thought to myself, *It doesn't
take too much to make Mama happy.*

We continued shopping but as I approached the cash
registers, I realized there was something I'd forgotten.
Of course, what I needed was located all the way on the

other side of the store.

"Mama, please stay here with the shopping cart," I said. "I'll run to the back of the store and be right back."

I dashed to the back of the store, grabbed what I needed, and dashed back to where I'd left Mama.

But, was Mama there waiting for me? No. I looked around the immediate area, no Mama. I started walking up and down the aisles, no Mama. I found my shopping cart, but still no Mama. I started calling her name as anxiety filled my body. Where was she? Should I have them announce her name over the P.A?

Finally, I found her sitting on a chair in the pharmacy department, with tears in her eyes.

"Why didn't you stay with the cart, Mama?" I exclaimed.

"I did. But then I took it to look at something and then I didn't know which cart was mine and then I just got lost. I'm sorry," she said as she looked up at me.

"Don't be sorry, Mama, it's okay," I said. *Okay, Linda, now you know you can't leave Mama alone in a store anymore.*

I feel bad and I feel sad that she got scared. Mama has always been really energetic and lively. She is still lively, but now in a quieter way. She can't be rushed these days and I must be sure to honor that.

**In the middle of every difficulty comes opportunity.**
*Albert Einstein*

*September 8, 2007*

Aunt Margie, Mama's sister, died. Mama was so very sad as we flew into New York. This really stuck her own mortality in her face. She was much quieter than usual on the plane, sleeping mostly.

We were only in New York for a few days and most of it is a fog to me. I have never liked funeral parlors. I hate cemeteries even more. There were relatives there we hadn't seen in years, and I was so worried about Mama. She looked pale and exhausted.

My brother David is like me. He did not go to the cemetery. But I did. David and I have always had a close relationship. I can remember changing his diapers and always being his protector. Neither of us can stomach hospitals, funerals or cemeteries. We both sort of burrow into our grief. We deeply feel it but we are also very private with it. I rode to the graveside with his wife, Kathy, while Mama went in the limousine with her sister and brother. There were six children in Mama's family.

*Aunt Lee, Mama, Aunt Margie and Aunt Alice (standing, l-r),*
*Uncle Joe and Uncle Billy (seated, l-r)*

Now only three of them are left.

Driving with my sister-in-law was soothing. She is
a special woman and a perfect partner for my brother.
Mama never tells Kathy that but she always tells it to me.
It was so nice to have someone drive me for a change.

When we were at the cemetery Mama whispered in
my ear, "Is this a dress rehearsal?"

*Not funny, Mama.*

The best day in New York was our last day. Daddy
and Heidi invited us to their place in Manhattan for
lunch. Mama sat in Daddy's wheelchair next to his
hospital bed and they bantered back and forth like

old friends. I guess they are old friends. Heidi said watching them together that day, she understood the relationship Mama and Daddy must have had when they were younger. I've always remembered the love they had for each other when I was child, and seeing them together like that was absolutely wonderful. It was a day I dreamed about for a long, long time. I felt a peace and happiness that was just blissful.

# *Still the Best Medicine*

*September 20, 2007*

Pat is here for a few days to visit with Mama and also so Paula can record a session with Pat and Mama together. The day after she leaves, David will arrive for the same reason. I am just delighted that we all have the opportunity to reminisce with Mama, and to spend time with her one on one.

*October 5, 2007*

Mama nominated me for the Square Cares 2007 Caregiver Awards: Most Caring Family Member. I didn't even know she had nominated me until someone called last week to tell me I was the second runner-up and would be honored at a ceremony.

She still continues to shock me. The funniest part is she told me she doesn't even remember what she wrote on the entry form. I wonder if her neighbors had anything to do with it. I have become friendly with quite a few of them since I am always over there. Many of them tell me that they wish I were their daughter.

This has me totally floored, though. I've been acknowledged by my peers and that's something, but to be acknowledged by Mama—wow, that is *big*!

I think sometimes we tend to forget that we really do have the power to affect change. Whether at home or out in the world, our actions net results—in more ways and more often than we think.

In that moment, I felt her silent but unmistakable message of love.

*October 12, 2007*

Tom's sister, Sue, and her boyfriend, Kerry, are here visiting. Sue has always had a special fondness for Mama. We had lunch in the dining room at Freedom Square and Mama was just thrilled to show off her apartment. She laughs and jokes like everything is just fine.

Pat says she doesn't think Mama will be with us for Christmas. I don't want to believe that, but I feel like everyone around me is saying good-bye to her.

Even my husband is telling me that I have to face reality, and Tom is a man of very few words.

*October 21, 2007*

I just got a puppy. She is my first. My niece Lynn

rescued her in North Carolina. I've named her Cash. After all, everyone needs a little cash (tee-hee).

About a year ago I decided I wanted a puppy. I know that I will be losing my Mama. And Cash will give me unconditional love, just like Mama does. Also, I can talk to her and she will just listen, not talk. That's a good thing!

Even Mama likes her, and that's a shock since Mama doesn't like critters.

Stephanie and her girlfriend Deirdre have been here visiting Mama this past week, and it's been totally enjoyable. Mama loves to have company. She always has. And the most wonderful part is that it gives me a little break.

*October 24, 2007*

Driving along on this glorious day, Mama—my co-pilot, was going on and on about the wonderful clouds.

"I know I say this every day, Linda, but these clouds amaze me. They are all big and fluffy over there and then just little wisps over there. I just love to look at them."

"I know Mama, they are spectacular."

"What do you think heaven will feel like, Linda?" she asked.

I was quiet a moment, then said softly, "I think it will be like the feeling you have when you hold a newborn baby."

*Bear with one another and, if anyone has a complaint against another, forgive each other just as the Lord has forgiven you, so you also must forgive.*
Colossians 3:13

October 31, 2007

Mama received a letter from Daddy today. They have been divorced for about thirty years. Daddy is not even able to write anymore. Heidi wrote the letter for him and he signed it.

Mama read the letter and handed it to me. As I read it, my heart was bursting with joy. It said, *"Dear Jo, I want to express my appreciation to you for the way you brought up our beautiful, loving, and caring children. It wasn't easy. I wasn't there. You did a wonderful job and I love you for that and I thank you. Love, David."*

I wanted to call Daddy and tell him how much I admired him. This letter was a precious gift to my mother.

Then Mama picked up the letter, read it again, and tossed it on the table. "I've got to frame that one. And the son of a gun couldn't even put a check in it?"

She cracks me up. I know Mama. That letter meant the world to her but it was definitely not something she was going to talk about. She doesn't know I know she tucked it in her purse later. Only important letters ever make it into her purse.

When I told Daddy what she'd said, he laughed. I am so proud of Daddy.

The happiest of people don't necessarily have the best of everything—they just make the most of everything that comes along their way. The brightest future will always be based on a forgotten past. You can't go forward in life until you let go of your past failures and heartaches.

***It's a great life if you don't weaken.***
*Jo McCauley*

*November 1, 2007*

"Linda, can't you get me a new body?"

"Mama, I'm going to find the doctor that made the bionic woman. Remember her?"

"Yes. She was pretty."

"And after the doctor makes you bionic, he will have to make me bionic so I can keep up with you."

Mama laughed. "Sounds good to me!"

"Are you drinking your Goji juice?"

"Yes, Linda Sue," Mama said in a very sarcastic tone.

Pat arrives today for another few days. She always has many medical questions for me and usually I don't have the answers. While she is visiting she will meet with the oncologist and also the hospice team that has been coming to see Mama. I hope this brings some comfort to Pat.

*November 12, 2007*

Tonight Mama and I went to a concert at my church. She has finally accepted that my church is right for me, and she actually enjoys herself there. We went to see the musical group Devotion and had seats in the first row of the intimate chapel. The lights were dim and the music was soothing. I just wanted to put my arm around Mama and hug her. So I did.

When driving home, out of the blue Mama said, "My mother has been winking at me."

I felt my heart skip a beat. I asked, "Did you wink back?"

"Of course I did."

Goosebumps broke out on my arms. I cannot bear to

look down the long road of years without my Mama.

But I don't have to. Yet. I have today and I intend to make the most of it.

*The teaching of thy mother shall be an ornament of grace unto thy head, and like golden chains about thy neck.*
*Proverbs 1:8-9*

November 14, 2007

Mama and I went to the Women's Celebration luncheon today. She likes the gals there and she loves the soup they serve. When it was my turn to stand up and say what I was celebrating, I said, "I am celebrating my mother. I am grateful for her and I love her." Mama had a smile on her face but she looked tired and just not well. I wondered if it was because of that patch she has to wear to help control her pain. Maybe it isn't working as well as it should.

On the way home she wanted me to stop for some groceries. Trips to the supermarket with Mama are now a project. She gets lost in the store, she walks very slowly, she can't carry anything. I told her I'd bring her home first and then get the groceries. She agreed, reluctantly, and when I pulled into the Freedom Square parking lot, Mama started vomiting. She couldn't open the door fast enough. It got all over the car and all over her. And by the time I got her out of the car it was all over me. Mama was crying and she was so embarrassed.

Two hours later we were both all cleaned up and Mama was sitting in her chair watching one of her favorite judge shows.

"Linda, I want ice cream," Mama said.

"No ice cream. It's too thick. I don't want you to get sick again. How about some lemon ice?"

"That sounds good, Mommy," she said with the look of a two-year-old.

This was the third time in the last month she called me "mommy." I don't like it. It gives me the creeps.

I decided to sleep over tonight and later, in the evening when all was quiet, I went out on Mama's balcony to enjoy the evening sky. I reflected and realized that, even with the daily challenges, the best parts are those tiny moments of joy with Mama—and I intend to not miss one of them.

Tomorrow I will call hospice and see what they can do to assist me.

*November 16, 2007*

Tonight Mama, Maureen, and I went to see the play *Cabaret* at the Largo Cultural Center with the Kiwanis. We love going to the theatre. When I lived in New York, Mama and I went to Broadway shows regularly. It was a fun night but Mama was subdued. She said, "I just feel icky." On the way out of the theatre Mama fell down. Maureen and I had to hold her up on each side to walk her to the car.

I am sleeping over again at Mom's tonight. She is feeling a bit dizzy. The nurse from hospice and I agreed this would be best.

This is all happening way too fast for me. I feel like I am suffocating. I ordered a walker and wheelchair for Mom today. I was not at Mama's when they were delivered. Mama refused them. When I found out and asked her why, she protested, "I do not need those!"

After five or six phone calls back and forth, hospice agreed to redeliver them, and left them by the front desk till I got there.

Tom and I came over to Mom's around four this afternoon. When we knocked on her door she did not answer. I came in with my key. The blinds were closed and the lights were out. It was dark, with the only light coming from the television screen. Mama was lying on the couch and she looked disorientated. A chill went up my spine. When Tom brought in the wheelchair and walker Mama got angry.

"I told you that *I don't need those*!"

"Yes you do, Mama," I said softly. "I want to have them here for you.

She only scowled at me.

"If you don't want to use the wheelchair, then I'll get in it and you can push me around because I am pooped," I added with a grin.

"Yes Linda," Mom said, then stuck her tongue out at me.

"What do you want for dinner?" I asked.

"Nothing," Mama said, her eyelids at half-mast.

She hasn't been eating much at all and that worries me. "How about a nice ice cream shake, then?"

"If you insist," Mama said, looking at me in disgust.

"Listen Mama, don't get mad at me. If anything, get mad at yourself because you are the one who taught me to take care of my family."

She scowled at me for a moment and then smiled.

I whipped up a shake with ice cream, fruit, and Ensure. It took her about an hour to drink it, with much humoring from me.

We watched an *I Love Lucy* video. We both laughed and laughed. I love to hear Mama laugh. I am so glad that Paula has been recording her these last couple of months. She tells me she leaves Mama's every week almost worn out from laughing so much. Although enjoyable, the laughter tonight did seem to soak up the last of our energy like a sponge.

I gave Mom her Tylenol PM and walked her into her bedroom. She is very weak and hung on me like a rag doll. I tucked her in like a baby and she whispered to me, "Good night and God bless." I gave her a kiss on her forehead, shut off the light, and went into the living room as the tears flowed from my eyes like a tidal wave.

"Good night and God bless." Mama has said this to me thousands of times, but tonight it was different. I felt like I was going to throw up. My heart was breaking. It is clear to me that Mama will not be around to say that to me forever.

*I will waste not even a precious second today in anger or hate or jealousy or selfishness. I know that the seeds I sow I will harvest, because every action, good or bad, is always followed by an equal reaction. I will plant only good seeds this day.*
Og Mandino

*November 17, 2007*

It's 7 A.M. and I am sitting on Mom's porch watching the sunrise. It is all so beautiful and serene. The big red sun rising. The sound of the fountain in the pond. The chatter of the birds and the ducks. It's all music for the early riser. The morning smells fresh and inviting. Life is good. Yes, life is good.

But that is not exactly how I am feeling. I am anxious. I feel like crying.

*Be strong,* I say to myself. *Don't lose it. Be strong, Linda, just like Mama has always been.*

Mama is sleeping in her bed. I go in and check on her every ten minutes or so. I don't want to wake or disturb her, but I do want to make sure she is still breathing. Funny, the last time I checked to see if someone was breathing when asleep was when my grandson Tommy was an infant. He could be such a sound sleeper that sometimes it would frighten me.

I feel like going outside and running around. Maybe in circles till I fall down. It's cool out. I'd like to lie on the cool grass.

Mom has become disorientated. She is getting weaker and weaker. I just want her to be peaceful and not agitated.

Last night she fell twice. She refuses to call me when she wakes up to use the bathroom. I am barely sleeping but she slips out of the bed so quietly, like a child on Christmas Eve trying to sneak a peek.

The wonderful medics from Freedom Square came to the rescue. The first time she fell, she was upset. She didn't want me to call for help but there was no way I could lift her by myself. I am so afraid she is going to hurt herself and take me with her. The second time she fell, she thought it was kind of funny. She was acting like a little kid. I just sat on the floor with her and we laughed till the medics got there.

The winding road of my life has led me right back home. I pause and listen for the inner guidance that speaks to my heart.

EVENING—I need a piece of paper to write on. Don't have my book with me. Guess it is time to start carrying it around.

I do feel so much better when I write. Like Mama, I realize there will be things I will not remember one day.

I always joke with her, "Sometimes I don't think it was so smart of you to move by your oldest child. 'Cause I am right there behind you, Mama."

We both laugh.

I am writing on the back of one of Dad's jokes. Thanks, Dad. Dad sends jokes to Mom regularly. I read them to Mama and we laugh together.

How is it going to be after Mama is gone? I am going to miss her so much. The closest person to me to die before this was my mother-in-law, Jean. She was beautiful, intelligent, loving, and totally non-judgmental. Whenever something good—really good, happens in my life, I always think about calling her on the phone. And in that split second I realize she is gone. And then I smile and talk to her without the phone. It's comforting, but at the same time there is an ache in my heart. I can't imagine what it will be like without Mama to talk to.

I am tired. Taking care of Mama is a balancing act of time, energy, attention, and caring. I have chosen to not whine and whimper about things I have no control over. It's the best response, especially when I'm pushed beyond my limits.

I hope I will be able to take care of her by myself. Last night my daughter's boyfriend had to come over to help me get Mama off the floor. He was a godsend. I am afraid if I call the medics too many times they will take Mama to the hospital. And that is the last thing she wants.

# *Someone To Turn To*

*November 18, 2007*

It's 2 A.M. I am at Largo Medical Center with Mama. This is the last place I thought I would be tonight—this morning.

Mama fell (actually, slithered) out of her bed onto the floor five times in the last twenty-four hours. First she is on the floor on one side of the bed, then the other. She is stubborn and I fear she has taken a radical turn. I can't get her up by myself—she is like a weighted rag doll. I am so frustrated, and worried at the same time.

Mama is so disorientated. The last time she fell on the floor, the staff at Freedom Square insisted on calling the paramedics because Mama told them her shoulder and hip hurt. Her shoulder always hurts—she's had arthritis in it for years, and I knew she had not hurt her hip. But they would not listen to me and insisted she be taken in for X-rays. I understand Freedom Square has procedures the staff has to follow, but that doesn't mean

I like it. Now we've had to drag her to the hospital and back for nothing.

*Patience, Linda.*

All day today Mom was talking about going to a wedding.

"When are we leaving for the wedding, Linda?"

"Much later, Mama."

"Where are my shoes?"

"I have them, Mama."

"I want to wear my heels."

"I know, Mama."

She also told me, very calmly, that she had squirrels under her bed. And she kept saying that someone took her grapefruit.

"Linda, she keeps messing up my papers. She is such a pest."

"She sure is, Mama." I don't know who "she" is.

"I hate when she messes up my papers," Mama says louder.

"I'll tell her to stop, Mama."

Later in the afternoon she looked me straight in the eye and said, "I have a daughter Patricia. She is a nurse."

I felt like saying *No shit, Mama.* Instead, I said, "That's nice."

I am glad I did my homework with Mama. One of the best books I read was *Final Gifts*, by Maggie Callahan and Patricia Kelley. It has really helped me to understand a bit of what is happening here. I just want Mama to be calm and happy, and not agitated.

We are still in the emergency room and she is giggling and telling jokes. I am exhausted—too exhausted to sleep, though, so I'll continue to entertain Mama the best I can.

Am I being a good daughter? Yes, I am. Always have been and will continue to be.

It's all so bittersweet. Yes, I guess that's it—bitter and sweet. Mama is happier than I have ever seen her in my whole life. Except maybe in Woodhaven, when Mama and Daddy and I were just three. Back when I jumped up on the sofa and told Mrs. Reggio not to yell at my mama.

*When we were just three ...*
*me, Daddy and Mama.*

Why can't her happiness last for a while longer? Why does she get such a short time to enjoy it? It all seems so unfair.

She's light now—gay, almost joyful. She's got the gratitude thing down. Gratitude is contagious and it is also a natural antidepressant. It did Mama good, listening to motivational tapes in my car over the last eighteen months. I just wish she could listen to them with me for another eighteen months.

Stephanie is on her way from Pennsylvania, thank God.

***Allow me to be a blessing to you and allow yourself to be a blessing to others.***
*John Coonley, cancer survivor*

*November 19, 2007*

Well, here we are at Hospice House Woodside. "Next stop, Woodside," keeps running through my head, like I'm on the Long Island Railroad.

When Stephanie and I got here this morning, Mama was in her recliner-wheelchair, down at the nurses' station. Mama has a urinary tract infection and she is very confused. It seems that last night she kept trying to jump out of bed. She pulled the alarm off, got over the bed rails, and ended up on the floor. She is still feisty as heck.

I still can't believe we are in hospice. We are telling Mama that she is in rehabilitation.

It is very nice here. Mama's room looks like a fancy hotel room—mahogany furniture, couch, TV, stereo, beautiful shades, and curtains. I just love the recliner-wheelchair. Stephanie and I took Mama cruising around in it tonight to check out the chapel, cafeteria, lounge, and other rooms. Mama wanted to go outside, but it was not nice enough. We promised her we would take her out tomorrow.

It is our goal to get this urinary tract infection cleared up and get our Mama back home!

*November 21, 2007*

Stephanie and I were here with Mama when one of our wonderful Certified Nurse's Assistants came in. She calls Mama "pretty lady."

"Is there anything I can do?" the CNA asked us.

"Can you do any tricks?" Steph asked. "Dance or sing…?"

The CNA laughed. Yes, we are a family of comedians.

I just wish we could take Mama home. Last night she looked up at me like a little child. "Please, take me home," she pleaded. "I promise I'll be good."

"As soon as we clear up that infection, Mama, and you get a little stronger, we will take you home. I promise."

I want to believe my promise. It breaks my heart to see Mama this way.

Stephanie and I decided last night that we are not leaving her alone. She is so disorientated and she keeps trying to get out of the bed. Even with all the bars up, with the alarm attached, and as weak as she is, Mama manages to jump out of the bed. We are afraid she will hurt herself, and we also don't want her to have to spend her time in a chair by the nurses' station.

When we told the staff what we wanted to do, they said that was just fine. They're extremely accommodating. So we're moving in!

*November 23, 2007*

It's 5:30 A.M. and I am sitting at home in my wonderful Florida room. I can't sleep. My mind will not shut off. Mama is in my mind every minute. It is as if a movie of our life together runs constantly on the theatre screen of my mind.

I have been sitting here for an hour now, like I am

*Robert with his "AP" grandmother*

in a coma. Daylight is slowly approaching, the birds are singing their wake-up songs, and a breeze is blowing gently. It's quite lovely, actually. I need to be outside more. Nature always makes me feel better, more connected and calmer.

Yesterday was Thanksgiving. The night before, my nephew Robert—Pat's son, came into town to see Mama. He is her only grandson. Since he hasn't seen his grandmother for some time now, he wants to spend as much time with her as he can. This is perfect timing, as it allows Stephanie and me to sleep in our own beds for a couple of nights.

Many years ago, Robert gave Mama the nickname "AP," short for "adorable and precious." Mama loves that nickname and is always telling someone about it. In fact, last week on the bulletin board in Mama's room, Stephanie wrote "Jo McCauley, aka Adorable and Precious." We will do just about anything to give her a laugh.

Thanksgiving morning Stephanie and I attended Mass at Mama's church, Blessed Sacrament. It was beautiful and soothing. The church was filled with little Pilgrims and Indians (except they're called Native Americans now).

Church has always been one of Mama's favorite places. She started attending daily Mass after her mother, our grandma Dean, died about forty years ago. Mama said that during her life when she was sad or stressed, she would go and sit in the church all by herself and pray. She said it was of great comfort to her. Her faith and devotion have always been her comfort.

When I was a kid I can remember opening our refrigerator, on many occasions, to find it filled with alter linens. Back before steam irons and wrinkle-free fabric, it was usual for women to dampen clothes and linens, roll them up, and store them in the refrigerator until they had time to iron, because damp fabric was easier to press. Mama was a master ironer. I recall often coming home from grade school to find Mama ironing alter linens in her bedroom, with a beer and some pretzels nearby, watching *I Love Lucy* and laughing out loud. When *I Love Lucy* was over, *To Tell the Truth* came on. Many times the four of us kids would watch that show with Mama and bet each other on who could pick out the imposters. Oh, life was so much simpler then.

Originally we had planned to spend Thanksgiving at my niece Lynn's in North Carolina. But since Mama is so sick, she and her family decided to come to us. It was such a blessing to have family with us for the holiday. Lynn took care of everything for Thanksgiving dinner. I didn't have to lift a finger and never would have been able to do it without her.

**Not he who has much is rich, but he who gives much.**
*Erich Fromm*

*November 25, 2007*

It's 5:30 A.M. My entire body is aching from being scrunched up on the couch. Mama had a busy night again, waking up about every two hours, not sure of where she is or what is going on. The room is dark and very quiet.

"WHAT DAY IS IT?" Mama asked.

"Sunday."

"No. What's the date?"

"November 25th."

"*Happy Birthday to you ... happy birthday to you,*" Mama sang softly, "*...happy birthday, dear Linda ... happy birthday to you.*"

"Thanks, Mama," I barely whispered, as the tears just flowed down my face.

I am not ready for Mama to leave me. I crept into the bathroom and muffled my sobs in a bath towel.

At 11 A.M., our wonderful CNA came into Mama's room with five other hospice staff members and a big chocolate birthday cake, all singing *Happy Birthday*. Mom was smiling from ear to ear and so was I.

*November 28, 2007*

Stephanie and I are both exhausted, physically and emotionally. It's hard to concentrate on anything but Mama, but we both still have other responsibilities that only we can fill.

Today we had a hospital bed delivered to Mama's apartment. Tom moved the furniture around to make things more functional. They also were supposed to deliver a tray, commode, walker, and wheelchair but I guess those will arrive tomorrow. Today I got a supply of adult pull-up diapers, bed pads, and latex gloves.

We were trying to get her released from Woodside

today but she developed a fever. As they explained to us, when she leaves here she will be off hospice. Then when we get her home, we can get home health care and rehab. Hospice does not do rehab—it is the end of the line.

We need to get Mama back on her feet. The longer she is in bed, the harder it is. We need to get Mama out of hospice. People are dying all around her and I don't know how much more Stephanie can take.

*November 29, 2007*

Rough night—Mama was talking in her sleep all night. I couldn't make sense out of most of it. When she woke this morning she said her mouth was very dry and it hurt. I swabbed her mouth and gave her a little sip of water through a straw. Immediately after that she started heaving, and the retching lasted about half an hour. I feel so helpless at times like that, but there is nothing I can do except stand beside her. She is now lying in bed exhausted.

My heart is breaking. She looks pitiful and weak. I just want to cry and cry.

The doctor says she now has a virus, so we're not going anywhere.

A clown came in to visit Mama and she perked up like her regular self. Unfortunately, I am finding it hard to convince myself that she will be coming home anytime soon.

Steph just arrived. I am leaving now and will be back later. The days are just melting into each other.

EVENING—Mama and I spent about an hour chatting after I got back this afternoon and now she is sound asleep. She kept asking me if everything was locked up downstairs. She also wants to know what time we are leaving to go out, so she can get ready. Even in her weakest condition she wants to go.

Mama just piped up, "What day is today? What is the date?"

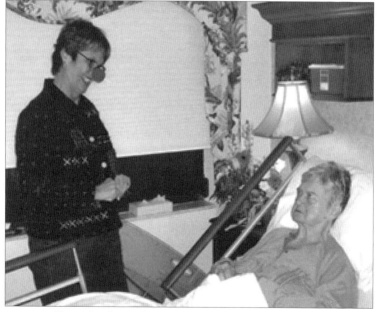

*Tears of a clown—keeping Mama's spirits up was my mission, even though my heart was breaking.*

"It's Thursday, November 29th, Mama."

"We need to get going with Christmas shopping. I am way behind!"

"Tomorrow, Mama."

I am so glad we're going to spend Christmas together this year. I looked forward to so many more Christmases with Mama. I have to accept this will be the last.

"Where is your dog, Linda?"

"At home."

"Bring her to see me."

"Sure, Mama."

I have learned that the difficult things in life are often the sweet things in life. I have learned that one cannot experience beauty without having experienced bitterness. I try to remember that I have to get through the thorns of the rose bush to experience the beautiful flower of the rose.

*The only people with whom you should try to get even are those who have helped you.*
*John E. Southard*

# *Dear Angel, Ever At My Side*

*December 1, 2007*

Mama has that glassed-over look, as if she's just staring right through me—and she is waving her hand like the Queen of England, with a faint smile on her tired face. Who is she waving to?

*Whoever you are, please pray for my mama.*

She doesn't want much to eat. She is too weak to participate in any of her care. She sleeps most of the time, just like a little baby.

Going over the past year in my mind, reliving it, is somewhat comforting. We had a good year, Mama and I. Lots and lots of laughs—many times just at ourselves.

*December 2, 2007*

2 A.M.—"Can you please help me?" Mama keeps murmuring in her sleep. She is very fidgety and seems to be in pain.

"Get me out of here, Linda!"

*Pat, Mama and Stephanie in hospice.*

Our special nurse, who makes special chocolate shakes for Mama to encourage her to eat, came in and administered some pain meds. They seem to last only for an hour or so and Mama's up again. I rubbed lotion on her legs and massaged them a bit, and then I read some prayers to Mama. I know she likes this.

I have this sinking feeling that Mama will not be able to come home again. She doesn't seem to be getting any better.

Mama began moaning and I could not understand what she was saying. I went to her bed and gently kissed her forehead. That seemed to bring her some comfort. She looked at me through squinted eyes, smiled, and went back to sleep.

"What time are we leaving?" Mama asked thirty minutes later.

"I don't know, Mama. I'll find out." I left her room, went to the kitchen, and made myself a cup of tea. When I walked back into Mama's room, she was sleeping again.

I am sitting on the chair next to Mama's bed, and I watch the vein in her neck pulse up and down. The sun is shining through the windows. Outside I can see the ten-foot-tall angel decorations.

It was several months ago that a dear friend suggested I read the book *Final Gifts.* The authors, Maggie Callahan and Patricia Kelley, are hospice workers—or saints, as I call them. They wrote the book to help us understand the special awareness, needs, and communication of the dying. I am more comfortable with what is going on thanks to this book. As Mama would say, "It's right on!" Pat also read it and Steph is reading it now. I am glad to have it here in Mama's room with me. I can open it up, read a chapter or even a paragraph and know that I am *right on*, that I am doing what is best for Mama.

*Dear God, I know you know when it is the right time. Just please don't let Mama be in any more pain,* I pray from my heart.

I am trying to be upbeat each day, but I am so

sad. Thankfully, Mama is not jumping out of the bed anymore, so sometimes when she is sleeping I go out and walk around. The grounds here at Woodside Hospice are beautiful, serene, and inviting.

When I first walk out the door, a part of me wants to run away. I stop, breathe deep, say a little prayer, and move. It is like walking myself into peace.

*I keep the telephone of my mind open to peace, health, love and abundance. Then, whenever doubt, anxiety or fear try to call me, they keep getting a busy signal—and they'll soon forget my number.*
Edith Armstrong

*December 3, 2007*

Stephanie and I need a break. I asked my friend Geri if she could come and stay with Mom for a couple of hours. Mama loves her, and she used to work in Freedom Square. When Geri walked in the room, it was the first time Mama perked up in about twenty-four hours. Mama was even a little bit of a wise guy with Geri.

Shortly after that an aide stopped in and asked, "How

are you today?"

"Good," Mama said. "Could be worse."

God bless Mama. One thing about her, when things are bad, she insists you don't let anyone else know—you just keep up a happy face. I have learned sometimes that is good but sometimes it is also bad. Stephanie and I have to be careful, as right now we both are vulnerable and emotional.

Our niece Traci also has been relieving Steph and me for a couple of hours now and then. Mama loves to joke with Traci and always says with a wink, "She turned out to be such a nice young lady."

Even Nicole's boyfriend has come by to spend time with Mama, to give Steph and me a break. Mama asks for her lipstick when she knows he's coming. That makes me chuckle.

Yesterday was Sunday. Steph and I both talked to Pat, no holds barred, about Mama's condition. She will be here Thursday with her husband, Wayne.

I'm really hoping Mama will be here for Christmas but I don't know. David and Kathy were planning on coming down December 26. I told him I think they should come sooner. Better a false alarm than not. When I told David that, he sounded like all the wind had been knocked out of him. He's the "baby" of the family, the youngest of us four kids. He said in monotone, "I'll call work and be there as soon as I can."

Tom doesn't know what to do. Emotions—yikes, not his strong point. I wrote him a letter and told him how sad I am and that I need to be comforted. I need to be held.

Mama can't hold me anymore.

*December 4, 2007*

A young fellow, another CNA, just came in to see if Mama was comfortable and if she needed anything. Mama was flirting with him like crazy. When he left, Mama whispered to me, "Boy, he is a real cutie!"

Yes, that's my mama!

I am grateful for Buddy, a social worker and team leader with hospice. He always looks people in the eye and there is a bond when your eyes meet his. He came to visit Mama this morning. Mama had a good night last night and, although very weak, she seems much more comfortable this morning. When Buddy arrived, Mama and I did our usual joking routine about anything we could find to laugh about.

I could see in Buddy's eyes that he wanted us to be a bit serious. He made a little small talk and then said to Mama, "Seriously, Jo, if you could have anything you want right now, what would it be?"

Mama closed her eyes for a few moments and

thought, and then she opened her eyes. Very slowly and distinctly, she said, "That my children will know that the Lord will take care of them and me. And it is my wish that their children take good care of them, as they have taken care of me."

That, to me, was one of the most profound things Mama has ever said. I just felt so blessed to be there to hear her say those words. Mama didn't say "I want to get out of here" or "I want to feel better." She just wants her children to be okay. A feeling of peace enveloped me as she fell asleep again.

Buddy and I walked out into the hallway. "She's ready," Buddy said, "when God is."

She has no fear, I thought, as my eyes welled up with tears.

**_People living deeply have no fear of death._**
*Anais Nin*

*December 4, 2007*

It's evening. Skylar and Tommy just left my house. I feel like I haven't seen them in weeks. They wanted to make Christmas decorations for Grandma Jo. We sat at the kitchen table and cut snowflakes out of different colored paper. Of course, after a short period of time, we had to get out the markers and glue—crafts just aren't the same without markers or glue, if you ask Skylar. They did a wonderful job and were proud of their creations. It was an hour of grandmotherly bliss, just what I needed.

Shortly before they left Skylar asked, "Why is Grandma Jo dying?"

I was taken aback and I had to think for a minute. I picked up my five-year-old granddaughter and sat her on my lap. "Grandma Jo is very old and her body is not working well. And when your body stops working you die."

"Does it hurt when you die?"

"No, it doesn't hurt when you die."

"Will Grandma Jo go to heaven with the angels?"

"Yes, she will, sweetheart."

Skylar looked me straight in the eye and whispered, "I don't want you to die, Grandma."

"We all die someday, honey, but I'm not dying for a really long time."

"After I graduate college?"

"Way after you graduate college."

"I love you, Grandma!"

"I love you too, Skylar."

I so, *so* love my grandchildren. They are gifts from God.

THE DAYS JUST seem to meld together. It is my turn to sleep at hospice tonight with Mama. I finally decided that I was tired of sleeping in my clothes. Since I don't normally wear pajamas, I went to the store today and bought some. It's like a lounging set, silky leopard-print pants and a jacket. Before Steph left, I went in the bathroom, put on the new pj's, brushed my teeth, combed my hair, and thought I was looking pretty good, actually. My best friend, Maureen, and Nicole were here also. When I came out of the bathroom, I walked over to the side of Mama's bed and asked, "How do I look?"

"You look like a cow in the pasture," Mama said.

Thanks Mama! We really needed a good laugh!

Mama is pretty feisty tonight but she has been complaining about her hernia. She wanted Nicole to look at it. We all know there is nothing we can do about it but Nicole and Stephanie both humored her.

Nicole pulled up Mama's shirt, then Steph rubbed Mama's belly and said, "Wish I had a watermelon!" Then Nicole put her lips to Mama's belly and blew a few raspberries. Mama laughed and laughed.

I know we are nuts, but it works for us.

*December 5, 2007*

Mama had a restful night, and has been laughing and giggling since 5 A.M. The skin on her legs is very dry and it is a little bit chilly in here this morning. I took the creamy lavender lotion and gently rubbed it into her legs. It soaked in immediately so I did it again. Then I put some nice warm socks on her feet.

"Oh, I just love that!" Mama said with the smile of a five-year-old.

Being in hospice I feel free to be the spiritual being that God created me to be. It is comforting. I recognize myself and the people who work here are sacred beings with whom there is a kinship. We support one another in faith and prayer, in word and action. As living, breathing miracles of life, we encourage, teach, and inspire one another along our individual spiritual paths, knowing these paths lead us to a greater awareness of God.

*December 7, 2007*

Hail, hail the gang's all here! David and Kathy flew in yesterday afternoon, and a couple of hours later Pat and Wayne arrived. I know they were all shocked when they saw Mama. The change in the past month is definitely dramatic.

Pat and Wayne are going to stay at hospice with Mama. I am just bursting with gratitude for both of them.

My heart goes out to my "little" brother. He is not much for words but his love for Mama runs very deep. When Mama still lived in New York, David would come by once a week to do his laundry. He's very picky about his laundry, and it gave him a little time to visit with Mama. He was always bringing her goodies from the gourmet deli where he worked.

Shortly after Mama moved here, he called her one day. He's as much a joker as the rest of us and told her, "I went by your house in West Hempstead and my key wouldn't work! I rang the bell and some strange lady answered the door and told me 'Your mother doesn't live here anymore! Go away!' So I just sat on the front steps with my laundry and cried."

*A family of jokesters from the get-go: David, with rabbit ears courtesy of me, Pat, Mama and Stephanie hamming it up in 1991.*

Mama would laugh and laugh when she told anyone that story. Oh, how I wish I could hear Mama's hearty laugh right now.

*December 8, 2007*

There is a beautiful living room/dining room at hospice. It has a fireplace and next to it is a beautifully decorated Christmas tree. That room is about the closest thing to home we have right now.

We decided to all have dinner there together tonight. I felt like I was in another world, though. Everyone was eating, talking, laughing, and trying to entertain Mama—like we always do. Mama sat at the head of the table in her recliner–wheelchair but she didn't say much. Except to tell Tom she wanted a cold beer! I was shocked, but I wonder why? He gave her a little sip through a straw and that was about all she had.

I was so wound up on the inside I didn't even sit down, let alone eat. I felt like we would never be together like this again but I just wanted to get out of there. It wasn't long before Mama started nodding off. I took her back to her room. When she was comfortable in her bed, I ran out into the garden to pray and cry and cry.

We took photos with Mama. When I look at them now, I can see how yellow her skin is. I should have known. Pat is always asking me over the phone about Mama's skin color.

*December 9, 2007*

I just found a penny on the floor in Mama's room. "In God We Trust." Thanks for the reminder.

Pat and Wayne had to go back to New York this morning. My heart went out to Pat. She was in so much pain and it was obvious that she did not want to leave.

I am feeling depleted and deflated. The energy has slowly leaked from me, like a balloon with a pinhole.

**Fix your eyes forward on what you can do, not back on what you cannot change.**
*Tom Clancy*

*December 10, 2007*

This is my worst night of all. I can't stop crying. I don't want Mama to leave me. She still has things to teach me.

*December 11, 2007*

Since Mama will not be home for Christmas, we brought Christmas to her.

Beside her bed are her huge fiber-optic poinsettia

and a scaled-down version of the nativity. Tiny live poinsettias dot her windowsill. Her room faces a beautiful courtyard that twinkles with hundreds of lights, and two beautiful, bigger than life-size, glowing angels watch over Mama from the garden. Talking about angels, the only decoration that is not here yet is Mama's favorite Christmas angel. It is still packed away in storage at Freedom Square.

I sent out Mama's Christmas cards today. We had started working on them at the beginning of November. I made up a variety of sample cards with different photos of Mama on them. She didn't like any of them, for one reason or another, so we decided to create a card with a photo on the front of Mama when she was a little girl. Inside it says, *The magic of Christmas brings out the child*

*Mama's last Christmas card carried one of the first pictures of her.*

*in me. May all your Christmas dreams come true. With Christ anything is possible. God bless you and your family. With love, Jo.*
It's a great card!

12:30 P.M.—A CNA and I just changed Mama's "fancy pants." She is like dead weight.

Dr. B told Stephanie and me that Mom's condition is irreversible. She said that Mama only has about a week left, give or take three days.

How can you just say that to someone? How do they know so precisely?

My reaction: go into the bathroom and throw up.

So here we are, near the end. I can't believe my ears. It doesn't seem real. Can't I wake up from this bad dream? I am sitting right here next to Mama. Can't she just be sleeping?

She looks frail. She barely speaks at all and she doesn't even want anything to drink. When she looks at me her eyes are blank. There is not even a hint of her beautiful smile.

I hope she can let go gently of this wonderful life and reach out for the new one.

2:30 P.M.—Nicole just left. She is heartbroken. As soon as she arrived, she crawled into the bed right next to

*Nicole and Mama had their portrait made on our cruise in 2007.*

Mama and, as she cried and cried, told her grandma how much she loved her and how she is the best grandma in the whole world. Mama didn't really respond.

Nicole and I took a walk outside to the beautiful gardens. I gave her Mama's wedding ring. Since Nicole was a very little girl, Mama told her that one day she would give her ring to her. Nicole was overwhelmed, and the two of us just held each other and sobbed. I felt a special connection to my daughter at that moment, and a feeling that Mama's arms were around me.

4:00 P.M.—I just put some cream on Mom's lips. She whispered to me, "Thank you. I love you."

Mama, I am going to miss you so, so much. The thought of life without you is absurd.

*December 12, 2007*

5:30 A.M.—Mom is growing weaker. She hasn't eaten much of anything this last week or so. Dr. B says it is just a matter of time ... perhaps Sunday. She suggested that we be honest with Mom. She said we needed to tell Mama that the cancer has come back and that she won't be getting better. She said we needed to assure Mom that we would be fine, and that it was okay for her to go.

A nurse and a CNA just came in to check on Mama and to change her fancy pants. Mama was moaning. They needed to turn her on her side, as she is getting bedsores. They did a fantastic job, as always, and now Mama is sleeping peacefully. She clutches a white teddy bear that Leddy, my minister, gave her.

11:15 A.M.—The hospice priest came by to say some prayers and to give Mama communion. Mama took only a speck of the communion wafer and a sip of water through a straw. Is this what she needed to let go? Will her next meeting with Christ be much more personal than this communion with Him?

Buddy and a staff member from hospice home care also came by. We all surrounded Mama's bed and prayed. As the tears flowed down my face, I felt nauseous. But I also cannot remember such tender moments with Mama since I was a little, little child.

My dad called Mama today. Steph answered. He said, "I just want to tell her I love her one more time."

Stephanie put the phone next to Mama's ear, and Mama could hear Dad say, "I love you." In her very frail condition Mama whispered, "I love you too." Then Dad said something else to her, she laughed gently, and went back to sleep.

*December 13, 2007*

It is all so surreal. I am sitting on the couch in Mama's room. There are Christmas decorations all around but it sure doesn't feel like Christmas.

*"Slee-eep in hea-ven-ly peace..."* is wafting from the CD player. Yes, Mama, I want you to be in peace.

I know we are in the final days, but are these the final hours?

Today is Thursday. The hospice staff guesstimates Mama will be leaving us on Sunday. I don't know how they figure that out, but everything they have told me and prepared me for so far has happened. *Wouldn't it be great if they were wrong this time?* I think as I look at Mama.

Mama is positioned sitting upright in the bed. Her eyes are closed. She is filling with fluids and her breathing is labored. She is not responding at all.

I want to crawl into the bed with her and hold her but she is not here. I feel like she has left us already.

They have Christmas ornaments here that say "Every Day's A Gift." In early November when Mama and I were planning what Christmas gifts she'd give, she said she wanted to buy some special ornaments to give to certain people. A little while ago I went to the lobby and bought sixteen of them. If that didn't have God's handwriting on it, I don't know what would. Knowing I'd bought the ornaments would make Mama very happy.

I am eating potato chips, my favorite junk food. They always have little bags for me here in the kitchen. Thank you, God.

I still think she is going to wake up and talk to me. Mama, please talk to me one more time!

MIDNIGHT—Tonight was Skylar's Christmas show at school. Since Pat is here again, we decided that both Stephanie and I would go to the show while Pat spent some time alone with Mom. The show was really cute, but instead of being a pleasant distraction it was disturbing. Mom should have been with us. Normally she would have been. Stephanie was visibly upset.

In this season I feel hope, and grief as well.

After the show Stephanie and I went back to hospice. Mom was out like a light. They had offered her oxygen earlier, as she was struggling to breathe, but she refused it. She didn't speak but Pat said her face was all scrunched up and she had an angry look. We all know Mama's looks—words aren't necessary.

Pat looked so sad and helpless. We three sisters hugged and then made our way to the kitchen.

Even though Mama was sleeping, we worried she could still hear us, and we did not want her to hear what we had to talk about. We talked about limos and flowers and all that other crap I didn't feel like ever talking about.

I am so grateful to my sisters for pushing me, these last couple of months, to make Mama's final arrangements ahead of time. "We need to do this *now*," they would tell me. "You'll never be able to do it at the end." They were right and I am so relieved that ninety percent of the arrangements have already been made. I am blessed to have the sisters I have.

Stephanie has worked with Blessed Sacrament Church on the funeral Mass. I want to do the eulogy. Normally, speaking is not a problem for me at all, but this will be Mama's funeral. I don't want to cry through the whole thing. Just thinking of it now makes me feel a little sick. We decided that if I am up to it, then I will do it, but we will ask Father John if he'll be prepared to do the eulogy if I'm unable to.

As I left hospice this evening, I sat on the bench outside. It was beautiful, clear, and cool and, as I looked up at the stars, I said a little prayer: *Thank you, God, for my siblings, and thank you for a mama who taught us all so well about being a family.*

It was 11 P.M. when I arrived home, tired but too wound up to sleep. I went into my office to scan more photos of Mama for her memorial video while eating creamed herring. Mama and I always enjoy creamed herring around the holidays. Mama said that if you eat it on New Years' Eve, you will have good luck. It's funny how food relates to your memories.

I alternated from crying to laughing, but it was a distinct pleasure going through all of our photos. It reminds me of what a great life we have had.

Looking at the pictures made me remember that Wayne hung the four communion photos of us as kids in Mama's room today. For some reason they have always been Mama's favorite pictures.

*December 14, 2007*

Pat and Stephanie have gone to Mom's storage unit to pick up her favorite angel, the one with the golden blonde hair. It is a dreary, rainy, nasty morning. I am waiting for them to get here, as I need to get home to work on a catering order.

I have been talking to Mama all morning even though she doesn't respond. Dr. B has encouraged us to keep speaking to Mom, as she said her hearing would be the last thing to go.

"Mama, wake up and sing one of your silly songs to me. Come on Mama, I'll sing it with you ... *A you're adorable, B you're so beautiful....* My voice was barely a whisper, really more like a low moan.

When I was a child I would sing the silly songs with Mama—all of us kids did. When I got a little older I just rolled my eyes when she sang them. When I became a mother myself I loved to hear her sing them to Nicole and now, and now ... I think the songs have ended.

We were hoping to get in touch with Fr. John today. It's funny sometimes, how small the world is. Fr. John is an old friend from New York who now lives here. Mama has adored him since he played together with all of us McCauley's as kids. Pat, Stephanie and I wanted to talk to him about the eulogy, but the phone number I have with me is wrong.

EVENING—Around 3:30 Stephanie called me while I was out doing business and errands. To her surprise, Fr. John had stopped by. He told her that he'd had other plans for the day, but he had this feeling of urgency to come see my mom, so he had his secretary reschedule his plans.

Stephanie asked him if he could celebrate my mother's funeral Mass and he said he would be honored. Fr. John took the phone and I spoke with him for a moment. He wanted some more background info on Mama, but he didn't want to talk on the phone while I was driving, especially as it was still rainy and nasty out. I was on my way to deliver a catering order so we decided to speak later.

I must have driven only another mile when Stephanie called again. "Linda, Linda," she cried, "Mom's dying *now*. I am going to put the phone by her ear—talk to her!"

"Mama, I love you, I love you, I love you!" I yelled into the phone. Maybe if I cried it loud enough she would not die.

Stephanie got back on the phone. "She's gone."

I stopped short. The carefully packed deviled eggs on the seat beside me slid onto the floor and all smashed together in their container.

As I pulled over to the side of the road, uncontrollable emotions started to shake my insides, erupting in waves of sobbing. I knew that Mama was now resting in the palms of God's hands. I could no longer clasp her aged, worn hands safely between mine.

What I hoped for, for so long, was now devastating.

Eventually I composed myself enough to deliver the catering order. When I got back to hospice, Mom was still in her room. She looked absolutely serene, angelic. She was dressed all in white, covered by a beautiful white blanket. Her favorite Christmas angel was shining in the room and Christmas hymns were playing softly. She was just so peaceful and beautiful.

And then I felt a moment of inner tranquility. I had prayed a lot that I would be able to feel this way when this time came. I was so grateful my prayer was so obviously answered.

Death is so *final.* Life is so *short.* Our lives are filled with "doing"—and yet our most common disease is procrastination. As if we will always have time to get around to "it," no matter what "it" is. Never more, in our time, has the setting of priorities been so important.

It is so true that, when our lives come to a close, what we may regret most are those things we did not do for ourselves or with our loved ones.

**Live so that when your children think of fairness and integrity, they think of you.**
H. Jackson Brown Jr.

*December 15, 2007*

My brother-in-law Chip did not arrive till late last night so he didn't make it in time to see Mama again before she died.

He did have a wonderful conversation with Mama earlier yesterday that I did not know about. He told me that he was at work and Mama was heavily on his mind. He said he was having this whole conversation with her in his head. It was so clear to him that he could even see what he was wearing in their "meeting."

He said Mama asked him, "Are you an angel?"

"No, Mama Jo," he said he told her, "I'm not an angel. It's me—Chip. But remember, the next time you see an angel, it's okay to go with that angel. Your children will be fine."

And that is exactly what happened a short time after Pat and Stephanie brought Mama her favorite angel. She went with the angel, to heaven. No coincidences in life, that's for sure.

# *No Goodbyes*

*December 16, 2007*

I don't want to think of Mom as having died. I want to believe she was birthed into a new life.

Mama, I miss you already. I just want to sit and talk and laugh with you.

I will never be able to say enough about the wonderful staff and volunteers at The Hospice of the Florida Suncoast. They are very special people who go above and beyond the call of duty. Never did I think that I would see a nurse kiss my mother, but I did. They treated my mother like she was their own.

Being so close to Mama on her journey has enlarged my view on life and death. I now choose to see death not as a wall but as a door.

EVENING—My grandson Tommy came by my side today and gave me a big hug. Kids are smart. I am almost always happy, but not today, so it was very evident that something was going on.

"Grandma Jo died," he said in his little boy voice. "She's your mother. She's in heaven with the angels now."

I looked down at him, feeling so touched—and the next thing out of his mouth was, "But Uncle David is coming to visit! Hooray!"

*Out of the mouths of babes.*

I just had to laugh, just as I knew Mama was right then.

*December 17, 2007*

When Mama died, a part of me died. I feel as if I am hydroplaning through this. The times I am saddest and, at the same time, happiest are when I watch the DVD celebration of her life that we had made. The music is great, the words are perfect, and in the pictures Mama is always smiling.

I try to do the same, but I grieve in the shadows of my smile.

There is a viewing at the funeral home this afternoon and again this evening. The thought of it makes me gag. I don't want to be there.

The tears I cry now are for myself. They are no longer for Mama, as she is at home with our Lord.

*For each life, there's a story, memories, and a collection
of moments that sum up the essence of the person.*
*Anonymous*

ào ♥ ●

*December 18, 2007*

I am sitting in Blessed Sacrament Church waiting for
Mama's funeral to begin. I close my eyes and, as painful
as it is, I am filled with joy—for I am in the presence of
God, right now. I am always in the presence of God, but
I often forget that.

I know a blissful joy that is independent of outer
circumstances and undisturbed by the pressures of
this world. I have joy that emanates from my spirit—a
joy that lives deep within me and originates from the
understanding that I am, right at this moment, in the
presence of God.

All space—within me and around me—is filled with
the Holy Presence.

I pray, expressing my deepest gratitude: *Dear God,
thank you for taking care of Mama. Thank you for answering my
prayers.*

*December 19, 2007*

We had a "Celebration of Life" today at my house. There were probably a hundred people in and out over the afternoon and evening. Everyone brought a dish. It is the first time I ever had people to my house and they all brought food. It's a Southern thing, I think, and it is wonderful. I am blessed by the support of my and Mama's friends.

The highlight of today was when Paula arrived and handed me the CDs with ten hours of Mama talking and laughing. Over the past six months Paula interviewed Mama many times, and she also interviewed Mama with Pat, Stephanie, David, Nicole, and myself.

One CD was a ten-minute compilation of Mama's stories and singing. We put it in the CD player but there were so many people here we couldn't really enjoy it.

It was around 11 P.M. by the time everyone left. I was very tired but after everyone else went to sleep, I lay in my bed in the dark listening to Mama talk to me. I know Mama will always be with me, but to have her voice is a true gift.

There is a CD titled "Jo McCauley/On Faith." Her faith sustained her through so much. Her faith in me was as unwavering as her faith in God.

*December 21, 2007*

I just came back home from Mama's apartment. Stephanie is staying there until she goes back to Pennsylvania on Christmas Eve. I choked up as I walked down the hallway, in a fog, to Mama's apartment. I needed to be there—to feel Mama, to smell Mama.

"Steph, I need to smell Mama's Red Door perfume," I said. As it came out of my mouth I couldn't believe my words. We all used to complain about Mama putting on too much perfume. When she would leave my house after visiting for a couple of days, we would have to air out the guest room. Even then, it would smell of her perfume for weeks.

"I don't need to smell it," Steph said.

"Well, I do," I said as I walked into the bedroom. There was the bottle, right on the dresser, waiting for me. I spritzed myself a few times. It felt and smelled wonderful.

"What are you doing?" Steph yelled.

"I'm taking over for Mama." I smiled.

After I left, I went to the dollar store to pick up a couple of things. On line at the register, an older woman ahead of me was chatting with the cashier. She took a little crocheted Christmas tree pin out of her pocket and gave it to the cashier.

"You look like you could use this. You are going to have a very busy day, I see," the woman said with a warm smile.

I could tell by the look on the cashier's face that she was surprised but also grateful.

The older woman said to me, "I don't get around too well these days, so I just sit in my big chair and make crafts. It keeps me out of trouble."

"That's good," I said.

"No it's not. It's a lot more fun getting into trouble." The woman giggled and walked away.

*That's exactly something Mama would say,* I thought. As I looked at the cashier I saw tears streaming down her cheeks and she blurted out, "That lady reminds me of my mom. She died last December."

"My mom died last week," I told her softly. I cried too.

With that the little old lady reappeared and said, "I think you need this." She handed me a crocheted candy cane and gave me a hug.

*Thank you, Mama,* I thought, and the tears just flowed and flowed.


*December 23, 2007*

"Change your mind, change your life." How long

have I been hearing this? But once again, like "Good night and God bless"—how many times did I "hear" that?

*Without loving and caring for others, most of us stand little chance of communing with God, no matter how many years we may spend in silent prayer.*
Bo Lozoff

*December 29, 2007*

Did some more packing at Mama's today. I was having a very emotional time. I looked to the heavens and said "Mama, give me a sign. Let me know you're okay." After I said it, I thought, *Linda, that only happens in the movies.*

I continued packing and about half an hour later sat down to take a break. I turned on Mama's television. *Crossing Over,* with the psychic John Edward, was on. At the very instant the sound came on, he said to a woman on the program, "Your mother says, 'Thank you for the journey!'"

I almost fell off my chair. I knew he wasn't talking

only to that woman. He was talking to me. *Thank you, Lord. Thank you, Mama.* I felt a wave of relief and gratitude wash over me.

As this year draws to a close and with a new one just around the corner, I realize what a turning point this has been in my life. Everything changes when your mother dies.

Life is *about* change! I am thankful for understanding that these changes are opportunities for me to grow. No matter how painful it has been.

*December 30, 2007*

When I walked into my church this morning I did not know it, but the service today was dedicated to all who had passed away this year. In front of the altar, there was a very long table with many photos of deceased loved ones. There were white candles

*I'll always remember Mama as a woman of beauty, in body and soul.*

everywhere and it made me think of heaven.

I took a photo of Mama out of my purse and placed it on the table with all the others. I felt numb. I cried through the entire service.

I was glad to be there—as always.

Peace, Be Still!

*December 31, 2007*

Today I brought my favorite alarm clock home from Mama's. I'd given it to her to use but she never used it as an alarm clock, even though she liked it. I had also bought Mama a clock-radio but she never used that as an alarm either. She preferred to have me call her in the morning or she would ask the desk staff downstairs to give her a wake-up call.

The staff at the desk told Mama a couple of times, when she first moved to Freedom Square, that wake-up calls were not part of their jobs. I told Mama the same thing, but she still kept asking them to wake her up. When they did, Mama would answer the phone singing to them. After a couple of times, no one ever again said anything about it not being their job. In fact, they said they enjoyed making the calls. Sometimes when Mama would walk me down in the evening as I left to come home, the people at the front desk would ask Mama if she needed a wake-up call the next morning.

Funny how things work out when you have a good cheerful attitude. I believe you can control your attitude or it can control you.

The staff all along has told me how much they loved Mama and her cheerful demeanor. They always say they would love to have more residents like Mama.

**Death ends a life, not a relationship.**
*Morrie Schwartz*

*January 2, 2008*

I miss Mom terribly. The loneliness in me stares out when I look at myself in the mirror. All the places we used to go together, I now go alone. I try to hide from the grief but it still finds me. Life will never be the same.

I don't want to give up Mama's apartment. It is safe there. It has always been safe at Mama's. Mama was never mad at me. Mama never judged me. No one will ever love me the way Mama did.

I can remember when I owned my housecleaning franchise in New York. Sometimes, if I was having a hard day, I would go over to Mom's. Most times she wasn't even there. I would let myself in and just sit on the couch and relax. It was safe and comforting and it would bring a quiet rest to my soul.

*January 7, 2008*

Bereavement groups can help you recognize your feelings and put them in perspective. They can also help alleviate the feeling that you are alone. The experience of sharing with others in a similar situation can be comforting and reassuring. They say that sometimes new friendships grow through these groups, even a whole new social network that you did not have before.

Well, we will see. I joined a group through hospice called "Adult Daughters Whose Mothers Have Died."

Tonight was the first meeting. We will continue to meet every Monday evening for the next six weeks. There were nine women there. It was very, very emotional. But also very, very cleansing.

I remember that my future lies in the people I haven't met yet.

What I have yet to discover is that joining this group is one of the best things I could have done for myself. I don't understand how anyone could get through such a time as this without the support of people who do understand.

*January 17, 2008*

I was at Mama's today. I was paralyzed, just sitting in her chair looking around, trying to feel Mama.

"Mama, please give me a sign," I said out loud, "a sign that you are okay."

A couple of minutes after I said that, I turned on the TV. John Edward appeared on the screen again and said, "Your mother says 'Thank you for the journey.'"

It was the exact same phrase I'd heard him say the other time. I know he was talking to someone in the audience, but it certainly worked for me.

*January 18, 2008*

We are moving most of the big stuff out of Mama's place today—the couch, curio cabinet, table, and so on. It is a totally gray day. The entire sky is just one big conglomeration of clouds. It sort of matches my mood.

One minute I am peaceful, the next I am sobbing. I will miss Mama greeting me at the door like a puppy dog always so glad to see me.

As I was sitting there feeling sorry for myself, I found a spiral notebook. Flipping through it, I discovered six different letters—from *men*—addressed to my mom! They are all dated December 1991 and each starts out "Dear Fun-Loving."

Each one is more or less an introductory letter. It was obvious they were in response to a personal ad! They are stapled on the left side of the notebook and on the right side Mama has all sorts of notes. I am assuming her notes were about conversations she had with these suitors. But being my devilish Mom, the notes are all in shorthand. Which I don't know how to read.

I laughed hysterically. One letter just had a big black X through it. *I don't need to know how to read shorthand to understand that one*, I thought. I doubt she ever dated any of them but I guess I'll never know. Oh Mama, you still crack me up.

When I told Stephanie about the letters, I found out that at the time she had placed a personal ad and convinced Mama to do so too, just for the fun of it. But Mama never let Stephanie know she got any responses.

That's Mama, still keeping us on our toes.

*Living consciously involves being genuine;*
*it involves listening and responding to others honestly*
*and openly; it involves being in the moment.*
*Sidney Poitier*

*January 21, 2008*

Going through all of Mama's belongings and packing up her apartment is just unbearable. I don't want to do this. I want to keep this place forever so I can be here with Mama. But going through her things does bring back memories, and it is my last act of love for her.

It has always been important to me not to be a burden to her. She was never a burden to me.

I telephone my aunts more often now. Mama used to give them the scoop on everything going on with us kids and now that's my job. One of my aunts said I am now the matriarch of the family and it is my job to keep us all together. When she said that, I thought, *Yikes, I'm definitely getting old!* I'm up for the job though. I am comforted to know Mama will always be with me, to help fulfill this responsibility.

I was astounded today when I found a card in Mama's stuff that I must have made for her when I about five. In my childish handwriting it simply said,

Some things never change, as I always say.

*January 29, 2008*

The most important thing I learned these last two years is to live in the moment. If I hadn't, I would have missed so much wonderful time with Mama.

In the past, I might be having dinner with someone and my mind would be racing elsewhere. Not anymore, I am clear and I am in the moment.

I can tell you every millimeter of Mama's face because I really looked at her, ever so closely, as the beautiful child of God she is. I can close my eyes and actually feel Mama's hand in mine, because I took the time to hold it so many times this past year.

I'm smelling the roses, and I'm hugging trees.

*February 2, 2008*

As long as I am able to remember, I will never feel alone, for deep in my heart I know Mama still lives on.

Today was Mama's memorial Mass at St. Thomas the Apostle in West Hempstead, New York. It was a beautiful, cool day. I was so nervous. I went through her funeral in Florida in a fog. Today I wanted to be able to keep my chin up. My throat felt like it was closing and I wanted to cry. I sat in the car in the parking lot and wept silently. I said a little prayer, asking Mama for strength and to get my fanny moving.

Looking out into the church, I was astounded. There were at least a couple of hundred people there to honor Mama. There were many friends and family members I knew, but there were also many of Mama's friends I did not know. As I was mingling in the church before the service started, people would come up to me and ask, "Are you Linda?" When I would say yes, they would ask me how my Mom's last months were. Many of them didn't even know she was so ill. I assured them the last eighteen months of Mama's life were filled with joy. I told them some of our adventures and they would laugh.

When Monsignor James Lisante came out to start the Mass he had a big smile on his face. "Normally when I am in the sacristy before a memorial Mass, everything is very quiet. But, not for Jo McCauley. It's like a party here with everyone laughing and walking around. Jo McCauley was definitely a force of nature!"

I had to smile too. Jim and I had been in high school together. He'd known Mama from the time he was a teen and she called herself "the Wicked Witch of Spruce Street" chaperoning at our dances. He knew her as a Eucharistic minister. He knew her devotion to her faith. It was comforting to know this man who spoke of Mama really did know her, and knew she really was a force of nature.

It was a beautiful but very emotional Mass. There was a gorgeous photo of Mama on an easel in front of the altar, and a glorious bouquet of flowers underneath her picture. I found out later that the flowers were from Maureen. On the card it said "From the 5th McCauley." I was touched.

At the end of the Mass we played the song *Mother, I Miss You.* Then Pat got up and read a poem she had written for Mom. It was wonderful. Following her, Stephanie got up and read a letter she had written to Mama. There was not a dry eye in the house. Next I got up to talk. I did not want to cry. Mama would want to see everyone laughing.

I mustered up every bit of strength I had. When I got to the altar I looked to the heavens and said, "Full house, Mama, and I'm on the altar. How cool is *that*?" Everyone laughed and I continued to entertain everyone with stories about Mama for a few minutes. I know Mama was proud of me.

We then had a lovely celebration with family and friends at the Elk's Club. Even Daddy made it there, coming in an ambulance. The best part was listening to everyone talking about Mama and laughing.

Yes, I am blessed.

***I have always grown from my problems and challenges,
from the things that don't work out.
That's when I've really learned.***
*Carol Burnett*

*February 5, 2008*

I am on a flight back to Florida and as I look out the
window of the plane, all I can see are large puffy clouds.
I swear I just heard Mama say, "Aren't they beautiful?"

Thanks, Mama. I love you. Please give me the
strength and clarity to go on.

Pat is coming down in a couple of weeks to help me
go through all of Mama's belongings. I am so grateful
for her. For some reason I think we've become closer
since Mama died.

I have a friend who says, "Sometimes the gifts we get
come in crappy wrapping paper." How true.

*February 21, 2008*

I want to do things that continue to honor my
mother, so I have decided to donate blood on a regular
basis. I remember when I was eighteen years old reading

in *Newsday* that a young girl was in dire need of blood. That was the first time I donated. Mama always donated consistently. "It's an easy way to help someone and it doesn't cost you a penny," I can hear Mama saying.

In fact, last month I found a letter from Mama's doctor in New York:

> *March 16, 2006*
>
> *To Whom It May Concern,*
>
> *Please be advised that Josephine McCauley is under my medical care, and she is a healthy 75 year old woman. Josephine is able to donate platelets on a regular basis.*
>
> *If you have any questions, please contact me.*
>
> *Sincerely yours,...*

When I walked in to donate blood, the nurse greeted me and said, "We haven't seen you in awhile. Where is your mother?"

"She died," I mumbled. The tears started flowing and I just wanted to go home, crawl into bed, and cry. But I stayed. I donated my blood, then set up an appointment to return eight weeks from now and left.

I know I did a good thing but I feel so alone. Everywhere Mama and I went together, I now go alone.

*March 20, 2008*

When I woke up this morning, I discovered there was

a leak in our roof. There was water all over the kitchen table and all over the business papers I had there, ready to take to my meeting this morning. My purse was also on the table, also soaked.

There was no time to do anything about it and I left for my meeting upset and angry. After driving a few blocks, I popped in a CD and listened to Mama laughing. Immediately my mood changed and I laughed too. Thank you, Mama.

*Gratitude unlocks the fullness of life. It turns what we have into enough, and more. It turns denial into acceptance, chaos to order, confusion to clarity. It can turn a meal into a feast, a house into a home, a stranger into a friend. Gratitude makes sense of our past, brings peace for today, and creates a vision for tomorrow.*
*Melodie Beattie*

*April 29, 2008*

I still feel just so alone. When will the tears cease? I could barely make my way into the diner for my Kiwanis meeting this morning. My feet felt like they were encased in cement. Mama is supposed to be with me when I go to Kiwanis. She should have been cracking her jokes and telling me to get her coffee or jelly or whatever her heart desired. I miss that.

It's funny how things that at one time annoy you a bit, you later remember fondly. I guess there is hope for me, as I seem to annoy my family on a regular basis.

Tears streamed down my face as we said the Pledge of Allegiance and sang *America the Beautiful.* I quietly and gently wept through the entire meeting. Just looking at the oatmeal in front of me made me want to throw up.

I am relieved that the people in our group are so loving. No one said a word but their eyes met mine with love and I got a couple of extra hugs on the way out. I haven't been to the last two meetings, as I was in New York, but I also realize I have been avoiding places that remind me of Mama. Just driving past Freedom Square can be painful.

When I left the meeting, I thought, *If I stand still, I know I will turn to stone. If I go home, no one will understand.*

I left the diner and drove mindlessly to the park. I walked, cried, and talked to Mama. I prayed for strength.

As I walked, I thought about things I want to write about. The writing keeps me connected with Mama. On the days I write, I'm okay. On the days I don't write, I am weepy.

When I decided to write, I looked to my mother for help, encouragement, inspiration, wisdom, and clarity. And as always, she has never failed me.

***I am who I am because of my angel mother.***
*Abraham Lincoln*

*May 2, 2008*

I have been to the cemetery a couple of times but it doesn't really do anything for me. Mama is not there. It is just a memorial. I think we are still having a hard time even believing that Mama is not here.

Up until now we had not decided what wording we wanted to put on the plaque. Today I talked with Pat. She had talked with Stephanie and David. They suggested that we put on it the words "Good Night & God Bless."

My heart is filled with joy.

*May 11, 2008—Mother's Day*

Yesterday I went to the cemetery to say hi to Mama. It was sunny and there was a slight breeze, just the kind of day Mama liked. I wanted to make sure that the flowers I dropped off the day before were in the vase on her mausoleum vault. They have to put the flowers in because it's too high up for any of us to reach. Mama just had to be on the top floor.

One thing I know for certain: my mother *knew* I loved her. Without conditions and without expectations. Oh, I was far from the perfect child, just as she was far from the perfect mother. But she and I had a special relationship. Even her death can't take that away from me.

Occasionally when I look in the mirror, I am a bit startled because I see that I am becoming my mother. But that is an honor. It's about more than getting wrinkles and having features like hers. I was blessed to have a loving, caring mother for such a long time. One of the many gifts she gave me was to teach me, by example, that we are all one big family.

I am grateful for my husband's support, even when my growth path doesn't make complete sense to him. It is a long, steep climb up the stairway of enlightenment.

I could write forever about my Mama. But now, I know, is the time to stop.

And at that very moment, after writing that sentence, a huge wind blew out of nowhere in the calm morning. An angel fell from a shelf across the room. Mama didn't need John Edward to deliver her message to me this time.

Happy Mother's Day, Mama. I hope I always make you proud of me.

# *Epilogue*

*Dear Reader,*

I am no saint. Far from it, but if, after reading this book, just one person is nicer to or more understanding of their moms, dads or whomever they have the privilege to be with at the end of life, it will be an honor to my Mama.

If you take anything from this book, please remember that reading about a journey is not the same thing as taking one.

I know how quickly the days, weeks, months, and years can pass. I know how easy it can be to find excuses for not beginning something new or for not taking steps forward, even if you can feel in your heart the need to do so. Don't let the word "tomorrow" slip through your lips. Take another look at your life. Count your blessings and give thanks. And above all, have faith in yourself. Be grateful for your ability to take action.

What if you had infinite knowledge at the point of your death? At that point, you could do anything you wanted, without fear because you would know it would all work out. But at that point it would be too late to take action in this lifetime.

So act now on what you know and believe, and trust in your beliefs. What is the one action you want to take before you leave this life? How can you accomplish it? What one step can you take toward that goal today?

Good night, Mama.

God bless *you!*

*Josephine Dorothy Bernadette Dean McCauley*
*April 13, 1929—December 14, 2007*
*and Skylar*

# *Thank You—Thank You—Thank You*

I am joyful and grateful and joyful and grateful and joyful and grateful.

Thank you to Dad and Heidi, my No. 1 supporters. Your unconditional love and constant enthusiasm inspire me to be all that I can be.

Thank you to my husband, Tom, for your support and understanding during my writing process. Your encouragement when I doubted if I could write this book uplifted me and gave me the strength to carry on.

Thank you to my daughter Nicole. My love for you expands every day as we continue to grow together.

Thank you to Skylar, my granddaughter and biggest cheerleader. Oh, how our journey has just begun! To my grandson Tommy, I am proud of you and love you from the bottom of my heart.

To my sisters, Pat and Stephanie, and my brother David, I thank God we are family.

To my oldest friend Maureen Petersen, thanks for all the laughs and for always believing in me. To my dear friend Lin Thornley, for loving Mama and for creating with me some of the best memories of my life. To my friends Jan Gidley and Carol Golgano, you have supported me in faith, word and action. To my Master Mind buddies, Diane Billman, Maria Ferraro, Terez Hartmann, Kathryn Morrow, and Joyce Pellegrini—I am a better person because of all of you.

My thank yous to Paula Stahel are never ending. Your wit and wisdom made this journey so much fun and so enjoyable. You silently challenged me and made me stretch. You honored my mama from the first day you met and shared your love with her. You took my words and buffed and polished them with love. You have guided me, taught me, laughed with me, and cried with me. You bless me.

To Jennifer Travis, for always walking beside me on my many endeavors with your beautiful smile and talents.

To my friend and webmaster Deirdre Cavener, your beautiful smile alone brings encouragement to my heart.

To my cousin and printer, Steve Kamp. You've made me feel safe on this adventure. Thank you.

To all the staff at Freedom Square ... thanks for making Mama feel at home.

To Dr. Saba, Dr. Feinman, and Dr. Hano for taking such good care of Mama and for encouraging her to laugh.

To all the staff at hospice who so lovingly cared for Mama, especially Cary, Denise, Nancy, Jody, Buddy, and Dr. Buck—thank you all. (P.S. Mama thanks you all too!)

# Books of Support & Comfort

*Another Country: Navigating the Emotional Terrain of Our Elders*—
Mary Pipher

*Chasing Daylight*—Eugene O'Kelly

*Death Benefits*—Jeanne Safer

*Final Gifts: Understanding the Special Awareness, Needs, and
Communications of the Dying*—Maggie Callahan and
Patricia Kelley

*Healing After Loss—Daily Meditations for Working Through
Grief*—Martha Whitmore Hickman

*Mothering Mother: A Daughter's Humorous and Heartbreaking
Memoir*—Carol O'Dell

*No Goodbyes: My Search Into Life After Death*—Adela Rogers
St. Johns

*The Last Lecture*—Randy Pausch

*Tuesdays with Morrie*—Mitch Albom